"Zhang Ruzhao, a talented writer, budding official, and avid student of Western thought, initially embraced the modern, secular lifestyle that was transforming early twentieth-century China. Then, finding it empty of substance and rife with suffering, she walked away. She devoted herself to farming, meditation, poetry, and the pursuit of a deeper purpose. Eventually ordaining as a Buddhist nun, Zhang went on to become a leading figure in the Buddhist revival, attracting thousands of disciples and devotees. In this remarkable book, Beata Grant translates Zhang's poetry and prose, which remain as vivid and relevant today as they were a century ago."

—BENJAMIN BROSE, author of *Embodying Xuanzang: The Postmortem Travels of a Buddhist Pilgrim* and editor of *Buddhist Masters of Modern China: The Lives and Legacies of Eight Eminent Teachers*

"A remarkable book. Beata Grant's translations of Zhang Ruzhao's twentieth-century earthy wisdom and care beautifully bring across the poet's subtle yet profound spirit and understanding, extending Chan's ancestral poetic tradition into modern times. In reading Zhang's descriptions of her daily life, and the poems her secluded years as meditator, farmer, and forest dweller inspired, I felt a true companion had been found."

—PETER LEVITT, cotranslator of *Yin Mountain: The Immortal Poetry of Three Daoist Women* and *Blossom Awakening: The Life and Poetry of Wandering Monk Saigyo*

"*In the Shade of the Green Willow* has artfully captured how Zhang Ruzhao, a Buddhist woman master, navigated the tumultuous years that sandwiched the Second World War. Reading it, I found myself repeatedly moved by the master's spirit conveyed through her own writings and by how respectfully and skillfully Beata Grant, being a renowned scholar of Chinese Buddhism and Chinese women, renders the nuances of those pivotal moments in the nation's long thought and cultural history.

The intimacy and authenticity conveyed through first-person voices and firsthand material are themselves precious teachings. I have no doubt this collection will become a classic and contribute to the English-language understanding of Chinese spiritual women and masters. It is a work whose wisdom belongs not only to its era, but to our own."

—REBECCA DAWN NIE, Chan master and cotranslator of *Yin Mountain: The Immortal Poetry of Three Daoist Women*

In the Shade of the Green Willow

Poems and Reflections of a Buddhist Woman in Modern China

Zhang Ruzhao

TRANSLATED BY

Beata Grant

SHAMBHALA

Shambhala Publications, Inc.
2129 13th Street
Boulder, Colorado 80302
www.shambhala.com

Cover art: Ma Yuanyu / National Museum of Asian Art, Smithsonian Institution, Purchase—funds provided by the Friends of Asian Arts, S1993.2 (Detail)
Cover design: Daniel Urban-Brown
Interior design: Anna Becker

9 8 7 6 5 4 3 2 1

First Edition
Printed in the United States of America

Shambhala Publications makes every effort to print on acid-free, recycled paper. Shambhala Publications is distributed worldwide by Penguin Random House, Inc., and its subsidiaries.

Library of Congress Cataloging-in-Publication Data
Names: Zhang, Ruzhao, 1900–1970 author | Grant, Beata, 1954– translator
Title: In the shade of the green willow: poems and reflections of a Buddhist woman in modern China / Zhang Ruzhao; translated by Beata Grant.
Description: First edition. | Boulder, Colorado: Shambhala Publications, 2026. | Includes bibliographical references
Identifiers: LCCN 2025051970 | ISBN 9781645474807 trade paperback
Subjects: LCGFT: Poetry | Creative nonfiction
Classification: LCC PL2832.3.H3576 .E97 2026
LC record available at https://lccn.loc.gov/2025051970

The authorized representative in the EU for product safety and compliance is eucomply OÜ, Pärnu mnt 139b-14, 11317 Tallinn, Estonia, hello@eucompliancepartner.com.

CONTENTS

PART TWO: *More Poems on a Life of Seclusion*

TRANSLATOR'S INTRODUCTION

The poems and other writings in this book, while they represent only a fraction of Zhang Ruzhao's complete works, offer a uniquely personal glimpse of the life and experiences of a Chinese Buddhist laywoman who in 1930 left an active life in the city and built herself a hermitage in the countryside. Zhang Ruzhao—also known by her dharma name of Zhang Shenghui and, after her ordination in 1950, Master Benkong—was born in 1900 to a relatively well-off family from Cixi, in Zhejiang province.[1] Her father died when she was just a child, and she and her two siblings were raised by a hardworking but conservative mother who arranged for Zhang to be married when she was only sixteen. Zhang's husband turned out to be an abusive philanderer, and before she was twenty, Zhang left the child she had borne him in the care of a relative and went to live on her own in the bustling port city of Shanghai.

Early twentieth-century Shanghai was a hotbed of social and cultural ferment as well as political and cultural unrest. China's Qing dynasty had suffered overwhelming military defeats at the hands of Britain, France, and Japan. After a period of internal rebellion and political turmoil, in 1911 it finally collapsed. Known as the Republican period, the decades between the fall of the Qing and the establishment of the Chinese Communist Party in 1949 were ones of continued political unrest as well as tremendous social and cultural upheaval. Although they actively resisted Western political domination, educated elites in urban areas such as Shanghai were eager to bring China into the modern age by embracing Western science and technology as well as progressive ideas such as the emancipation of women. Zhang Ruzhao was determined to take full advantage of some of the new opportunities for women to acquire an education beyond the most basic and, after many setbacks, earned a college degree in English literature in 1925. By this time, she had also made a place for herself in Shanghai's vibrant literary world and published her first collection of poetry. Although she would go on to write many essays and scholarly articles, it is as a poet that she first made her mark. Although she would later lament what she refers to as her poetic "addiction," she never stopped writing verse, and her later poetry shifted primarily to include Buddhist themes.

During the early 1920s, Zhang was also actively engaged in the political movements that rocked Shanghai and other urban centers. At one point she was even thrown in jail after participating in a student protest. An ardent advocate of women's rights, Zhang, after graduating from college, made plans to go to the United States to study the position of women, but she had to abandon the idea when her family put up a strong opposition. She had overcome many obstacles up to this point, but this particular setback sent her into a deep depression. She would later write that she wept so hard that she nearly went blind.

In 1926, still deeply committed to bringing about change in her country, she took an entry-level position at a local office of the Nationalist Party of China (Guomindang). At first she saw this as an opportunity to put her talents to use in the service of her country, but soon she grew profoundly disillusioned with the corruption and political infighting around her and resigned in disgust. Later, in her "Verses on Returning to the Land," she would point to this experience as one of the main reasons for her decision to move to the countryside.

In 1927, Zhang was invited to oversee the organization of the new Ningbo municipal library. It was a full-time job with many responsibilities, but every spare moment would find her taking advantage of the opportunity to read widely in Western and Chinese literature, history, and philosophy and to think deeply about herself and her times. By 1930, Zhang had become thoroughly disillusioned with what she saw as society's often mindless embrace of everything and anything new and modern. She was also acutely aware of the suffering and spiritual emptiness she experienced in her own life and sensed in the lives of many others. As she had attended Christian schools and counted a number of sympathetic missionaries among her closest friends, she even looked into becoming a Christian herself. However, after these years of intensive study and thought, Zhang found herself increasingly drawn more to traditional Chinese philosophies and religions and, above all, to Buddhism.

At a time when many educated elites saw traditional Chinese religion as a major impediment to modernization, a number of influential Chinese Buddhist monks and laypeople knew that they would have to do something if they were to continue to be of relevance. Some, like the charismatic and progressive Master Taixu (1890–1947), advocated far-reaching reforms. Others, such as the Pure Land master Yinguang (1891–1940), focused instead on reaching out to a more urban elite audience by making uses of advances in printing and publishing. Indeed, a vital component of this Buddhist revival was education, including the establishment of Buddhist seminaries for both monks and nuns. Zhang

Ruzhao was very much influenced and inspired by these leaders and would eventually make important contributions to this revival as a writer and an educator.[2] At this point, however, she was at the early stages of her spiritual journey—although she felt enough of an affinity to Buddhism to have taken refuge in 1928 with Pure Land Master Yinguang.

In 1930, Zhang turned thirty, an important transition point in many people's lives, and she was desperate to make a change in hers. It was at this time that she found and purchased a small property located just north of her hometown of Cixi. The land backed up to Mount Kan, at the foot of which was the scenic Lake Ci.[3] It had also once been the retirement retreat of a famous sixteenth-century scholar-official. Zhang felt it would be an ideal place for her to heal from the trauma of the previous decades and, even more important, pursue her growing interest in religious study and practice. She named her retreat Gaya Farm-Forest (*Gaya nonglin*)[4] because, as she would later explain, its location—not in the city but also not completely isolated—reminded her of descriptions in the Buddhist scriptures of the holy city of Gaya and nearby Mount Gayashirsha.[5] She then set out to clear the weeds and debris and restore what ramshackle buildings remained on the property. Determined to be as self-sufficient as possible, she also planted fruit trees and vegetable gardens.

In so doing, she was inspired by Master Taixu's advocacy of "farming-Chan" (*nongchan*), a concept based on the principle of "a day without work is a day without food" that is traditionally attributed to the Tang dynasty Chan master Baizhang Huaihai (720–814). Farming-Chan was designed to counter the popular perception that monastics were parasites on society.[6] Some of the more progressive monasteries at the time were beginning to make farming a more integral part of the monks' daily routines, but for a single woman who was not a monastic to undertake this way of life was unusual, to say the least.

It is clear from Zhang's "Verses on Returning to the Land" that she also saw herself as part of a long Chinese tradition whereby an official would leave his post, whether because he had reached the age of retirement or in protest against a corrupt government, and return to his hometown to pursue a simpler life. This life might consist of farming, but it also allowed ample time for intellectual and artistic pursuits such as reading, calligraphy, painting, and strumming the zither—activities that Zhang engaged in as well. One of the most famous examples of this is the poet-recluse Tao Yuanming (365–427), who quit his job because he was unwilling to scrape and bow for a meager "five pecks of rice." He later wrote poetry that celebrated a life of hoeing beans, reading for pleasure, and sharing a convivial jug of wine with his country neighbors.

In traditional China, only men could hold official posts, and thus only men could leave them to become recluses. This lack of female models did not deter Zhang. In fact, she even implicitly compares her self-exile to Confucius leaving his home state of Lu because of its corrupt ruler. She also compares herself with Bodhidharma, traditionally regarded as the first patriarch of Chan Buddhism, who after a fruitless discussion with Emperor Wu at his southern court crossed the Yangzi River and went north, where he spent nine years in silent meditation in a mountain cave. Even as a young girl, Zhang was also particularly fond of the poetry of Hanshan, or Cold Mountain (late eighth–early ninth century), the elusively eccentric Buddhist hermit-poet whose translated works are familiar to many Western readers.

It would be hard to blame some of Zhang's detractors for thinking that she was trying to set herself up as an equal to these famous men of the past. Zhang herself, however, insisted that she was "neither a poet nor a Chan master" and that her primary aspiration was to get to the source of all the sorrows and anxieties both within herself and in so many people around her. Indeed, while many of Zhang's verses describe what seems to be a near-idyllic life, others speak of an ongoing and often fierce personal struggle with persistent negative habits, anxieties, and attachments. At first she appears to be primarily inspired by the example of neo-Confucian thinkers such as Yang Jian (1141–1225), who, like Zhang, was a native of Cixi. Yang Jian was one of the most important followers of Lu Jiuyuan (1139–1193), also known as Lu Xiangshan, the founder of the neo-Confucian School of Mind (*Xinxue*). Like Lu, Yang held the view that the heart-mind (*xin*) was endowed with an innate knowledge of the (intrinsically good) universal principle (*li*) by means of which a person could realize their oneness with all things. In this, Yang was partly influenced by Chan Buddhist notions of the equivalence of the human heart-mind with Buddha or Buddha nature, which is why Zhang, in one of her verses, would refer to him as "a Chan master inside, outside a famous Confucian." Yang Jian also practiced a form of deep contemplation that led to an experience of awakening akin to that described in so many Chan texts, and that Zhang refers to in her writings. However, in the end Zhang's primary interest was in Buddhist rather than neo-Confucian practice.

During her first years living at Gaya, Zhang engaged in a form of intensive Chan meditation associated primarily with the Linji (Rinzai) school of Chan Buddhism. This practice requires that the meditator grapple intensively on a *huatou* or "critical phrase," such as "Who was I before my mother and father were born?"[7] In attempting to find an answer to this question, meditators, forced to face the limitations of the purely intellectual or rational mind, find themselves in a deeply existential and often very painful quandary, which, if all goes well, is finally resolved in a direct and unmediated insight into their inherent Buddha nature. This type of meditation is often described in terms of a battle against the forces of ignorance from which one aspires to emerge victorious. Although Zhang admits to having benefited greatly from this practice, she found it to be detrimental to her health and turned to more gentle and gradual forms of meditation, as well as to practices such as sutra study and recitation. She continued, however, to be guided by the examples of eminent Chan masters of the Yuan and Ming dynasties such as Zhongfeng Mingben (1263–1323), Gaofeng Yuanmiao (1238–1295), Hanshan Deqing (1546–1623), and Zibo Zhenke (1543–1603), with whose records she was deeply familiar and from which she often quotes.

By 1933, Zhang Ruzhao had firmly embarked on the Buddhist path. While her practice during her first couple of years at Gaya Farm-Forest had been relatively solitary, she now began to actively seek guidance from a wide range of Buddhist teachers, both monastic and lay. Among her teachers was Master Taixu, from whom she received the dharma name Shenghui (Peerless Wisdom) and at whose request she wrote a piece entitled "I Believe in Buddhism," first published in 1933. She also continued to write and publish, although now her topics were primarily Buddhist-related: *The Seafoam Collection* (*Haiou ji*), a collection of poetry, was published in 1934; and *Prajna Flowers* (*Bore hua*), a collection of poetry and prose, was published the following year. She was never completely isolated, as she maintained close connections with a wide circle of friends, relatives, and monastics with whom she would often exchange letters and poems. Many would also come to seek her out at Gaya.

Buddhist education for women had always been a cause close to Zhang's heart, and she was overjoyed when in 1937 she was invited to teach at the first Buddhist seminary for nuns just established in Zhejiang province. Only nine months after her arrival, however, the seminary closed due to the outbreak of the Second Sino-Japanese War, sometimes referred to as the "Asian holocaust," which raged from 1937 to 1945. Zhang took refuge at Gaya Farm-Forest for the duration of the war. As we can see in later poems such as "Living in the Forest: Reflections," she endured many hardships during this period and often found herself isolated by circumstances rather than choice.

While Zhang studied with teachers from different schools of Buddhism, ultimately she felt the greatest affinity with the school of Tiantai Buddhism, which incorporated many elements of both Chan and Pure Land, and offered a comprehensive and integrated system of teaching and practice.[8] During this period, Tiantai Buddhism was also experiencing a major revival, thanks especially to the active leadership of Master Dixian (1858–1932), known for the Guanzong Lecture Temple in Ningbo, an important center of modern Buddhist education in Ningbo. He also founded the *Periodical of the Dharma Propagation Society* (*Hongfa shekan*), which was primarily dedicated to the promotion of Tiantai thought. Zhang's pieces often appeared in this journal, including "A Note on Gaya Farm-Forest," published in 1933. In 1936 she had become a formal disciple of another of Dixian's students, Master Genhui (1881–1951), after which she was often invited to lecture at the Guanzong Lecture Temple. Her commitment to Tiantai deepened, and in 1949 Master Genhui invited her to take up residence at the Miaoyin Hermitage—which had been his own personal retreat—where she could practice and receive students. Finally, in 1950, Zhang decided to become ordained as a nun. Not long afterward, Master Genhui, who would pass away the following year, also named her as one of his dharma heirs, the only woman among several men.

Over the next several years, Zhang, now known as Tiantai Master Benkong (Original Emptiness), attracted many disciples and thousands of devoted lay followers. Several of these followers took it upon themselves to put together *The Misty Waters*

Collection (*Yanshui ji*), the fourth and final collection of Zhang's writings, which was published in 1953. After this time, although she wrote less, Zhang traveled and lectured widely in southern China, and in 1954 and 1956 she visited Japan and India. By the end of the decade, however, the new Communist regime had begun to forcefully impose its ideological constraints on religious activities, including forcing monastics to return to lay life.

In 1959 Zhang had to leave her convent, which was turned into a factory and then later a military storage site. Unfortunately, we do not know very much about her life after this, although it appears that she adamantly refused to stop wearing her monastic robes. We do know that during the early years of the Cultural Revolution (1966–1976), Zhang was subjected to particularly harsh treatment, perhaps because of her previous association with the Nationalist government, and that she passed away in 1969. No trace remains today of Gaya Farm-Forest, which was sold by Zhang's family shortly after her ordination. The Miaoyin Hermitage, however, was restored and expanded in 1985 and is today an active convent. In 2019, a celebration was held there in commemoration of the fiftieth anniversary of Zhang's death. The participants not only made offerings of incense at the altar but also sat down to write their own poems and couplets in her memory, a testimony to the enduring inspiration of her writings.

A Note on the Translations

Many of Zhang's early twentieth-century contemporaries sought to make a radical break with the past by writing primarily in vernacular Chinese (*baihua*) rather than classical Chinese (*wenyan*) traditionally used by educated elites. Zhang too makes use of the vernacular to write her essays and articles, which were designed for a broad audience rather than a select few. Nevertheless, while some of these same contemporaries also adopted Western poetic forms such as free verse, Zhang chose to adhere to the age-old conventions of classical Chinese poetry, which include very specific rules regarding such things as poem length, number of characters (words) per line, and rhyme. An accomplished poet, Zhang could write in all of the different forms or genres of classical Chinese, although the majority of the poems she wrote about her life at Gaya Farm-Forest were four-line verses, often used as well for Chinese Buddhist religious verse, or *gatha*. In these poems, each line comprises seven (or in some cases, five) characters, with a rhyme at the end of the second and fourth lines. Often these short poems are written as part of a loosely linked series, which helps to offset their brevity.

Zhang also made use of other traditional poetic forms, including *gushi* (ancient-style poetry) and *lushi* (regulated verse). Gushi requires five characters per line, with rhymes at the end of each alternate line. However, it allows for considerable latitude in terms of the number of lines per poem, which is why it was often used for historical or autobiographical poetic narratives, such as Zhang's "Verses on Returning to the Land." Lushi stipulates a length of precisely eight lines, each of which comprises either five or seven characters, and which had strict requirements regarding such things as rhyme. The last three poems in this book were all written in this form.

In translating Zhang's writings, and in particular her poems, I have endeavored to retain as much form of the original as possible. Except for the rhymes, which rarely translate happily, I have also tried to be as faithful as possible to the language and spirit of the original. Classical Chinese poetry, largely due to its concise nature, often makes use of allusions to people, events, and texts from the past, most of which would be recognized by readers familiar with the Chinese literary tradition (or the Buddhist scriptural one). Highly educated and well read, Zhang also makes use of allusions in her writing, for which I have tried to supply explanatory notes that add rather than hinder the reader's appreciation. It is worth noting, however, that Zhang did her best not to use too many erudite allusions. Indeed, she very candidly admits that she did not expend a great deal of effort polishing and perfecting her writing. “I write when I feel inspired to do so,” she tells us, “but immediately after having written something, I put it aside without thinking about it anymore. Nor do I worry in the slightest about whether the wording is skillful or clumsy, or the parallelism is smooth and regular. All I try to do is shed some light on the truth; I have no desire to be showy or flamboyant.” Moreover, like many deeply committed Buddhists before her, Zhang often expressed an ambivalence about what she calls her “addiction” to poetry, which she felt sometimes conflicted with her practice of the Dharma. Indeed, after her ordination, she apparently asked her disciples to destroy her poetic writings, a request that thankfully they ignored.

PART ONE

The Gaya Farm-Forest

VERSES ON RETURNING TO THE LAND

I

In my early twenties, I was fond of writing;
I studied and I aspired to the highest ideals.
As the country's affairs were in total chaos,
I took up a post hoping to help restore order.
I paid close attention to investigating things,
And worried over military and political affairs.
As someone long devoted to her country,
I often found myself weeping in sorrow.
It was when I turned twenty-seven
That I first tried out the official life.
But I noticed how so many people

Were interested only in themselves,
Oblivious to the people's suffering,
Lusting only after wealth and power.
I truly wanted to make a contribution,
But my lowly status made that hard.
Besides, being frank and foolhardy,
I was also shunned by my colleagues.
In truth, I brought trouble on myself;
Currying favor was not my ambition.
Over the course of a number of years,
My courage and loyalty were all gone.
I left and I returned to my hometown
To take up a hoe, learn to work the land.[1]

2

Adversity and prosperity are unavoidable,
Successes and failures follow circumstances.
Having come to fully understand politics,
It was right to return to my original nature.
In a swift current, it's best to bravely retreat;
To hesitate would only be putting things off.
Flowers bloom knowing they will wither,
Why wait until spring comes to a close?
Money and titles cannot be relied on,
For they will vanish like morning dew.
No need to be envious of immortals:
Whose abstinence brings only pain.
The road to Chang'an is very long
And so dusty that one cannot linger.
The Penglai mountain is barely visible,
Shrouded in mist and floating clouds.
Hidden fish are happy in clear waves,
Exotic birds choose the greenest trees.
Confucius left for the state of Qi,
Bodhidharma crossed on a reed.
Walking, walking, again walking,
Once you leave, do not look back.[2]

3

Unwilling to grovel for a meager wage,
I finalized plans to return to the land.
Calmly I went back to my old home,
Purchased a cart and a sturdy ox.
The sunset brings mist over the fields,
A spring rain good for a first plowing.
My garden full of peaches and plums,
Orchids, mums, a row of parasol trees.
Backed by Mount Kan in the north;
Surrounded by Lake Ci in the south.
Relatives and friends happily conversing;
Poetry and history books for reading up.
When in high spirits, I take a bottle of wine
And listen to orioles sing in the hidden valley.
The world of politics is turmoil and trouble.
At first you laugh, and then you weep.
I've been fortunate to return to the land.
How could I not know how lucky I am?
I delight in being poor but upright;
What need have I for a fat salary?
Mugwort and mums suffice for meals,

Lotus leaves will be fine for clothes.
I do whatever it is I feel like doing:
Singing with my countryfolk friends.[3]

A NOTE ON GAYA FARM-FOREST

Mount Fubi (Mount Floating Emerald) is situated in the northern corner of Cixi. Winding down from a fork in the Shici Ridge (Stone Thorn Ridge), it slopes down into the county seat, then rises up majestically before quietly falling away; this is why it is also called Mount Xianhou (Behind the County). In the Ming dynasty (1368–1644), a high-ranking official named Feng had a retirement place built for himself at the eastern foot of the mountain, with pavilions and terraces surrounded by walls, trees, bamboo, and flowers.[1] After the fall of the dynasty, this scenic spot fell into neglect and disrepair and was rarely visited. Over the next few centuries, the ravages of war and turmoil turned it into even more of a wasteland. Toward the end of the Qing dynasty (1644–1911), some of Feng's descendants restored the site, renaming it Tao's Garden, and for a time it saw a constant stream of visitors.[2]

In the summer of 1930, I happened to pass by the place and saw that it had once again fallen into disrepair, and its few remaining flowers and trees were overgrown with weeds. The walls of the building, which had been rented to some vegetable vendors, were just about to collapse. Filled with sadness at the vicissitudes of human affairs and how this once beautiful place had become so desolate over the decades, I purchased it for fifteen hundred gold coins. The land up to the mountain is densely wooded but still close to the town. Because this is how Gaya Mountain and Gaya City are described in the scriptures, I affectionately named it Gaya Farm-Forest. Repairing the walls, replacing the beams, and whitewashing the rooms, I turned the building into a modest retreat for reading and study. I then cleared and burned all the weeds and deadwood, allowing the fine trees and trimmed bamboo to fully emerge and happily flourish. Taking into consideration the terrain, I planted more than a hundred fruit trees, including peach, apricot, plum, pear, tangerine, and pomelo, in the hope that they would thrive and one day bear fruit to gather and pick for the enjoyment of my guests, which would be a true delight!

My living quarters consist of no more than five bays, my land of no more than ten *mu* (about 1.5 acres), and the hill that backs it no more than nine *ren* (about seventy-two feet) high. Gone are the splendid pavilions and terraces and the secluded corridors and moon pavilions, as are the elegant gatherings with their music, games of chess, and wine. And yet my life here has been one of carefree leisure. With paintings to my left and books to my right, singing songs in the morning and chanting poems in the evening, I am happy and content, far away from the chaotic clamor and fickle changes of the world. Before the wind gusts and after the rain falls, I slip on my clogs and climb up to a high spot from where I can gaze at Mount Kan dripping with rich green, and Lake Ci as clear as a mirror.[3] On the left bank of the lake stands a building set among tall, towering trees, which is where Master Yang, a person that in my heart I have always admired, used to deliver his lectures at Lake Ci.[4] One finds there also the tombs of Minister Yao and Woman Martyr Jin.[5] Although now covered with vines and knee-deep in weeds, the enduring reputation of their noble characters and sterling integrity continues to this day. I admire them greatly and am ashamed that I've barely begun to live up to their examples. There is an old saying: "No matter how high a mountain is, only if there is an immortal living there will it become famous."[6] My mountain may be just a humble hill, but I am fortunate to be living in such proximity to famous ministers, erudite scholars, filial sons, and virtuous wives of the past, whose fragrant memory continues undiminished. Here I can be friends with the ancients and forget about the gains and losses, the rise and fall of worldly affairs.

EXPERIMENTS IN A LIFE OF FARMING-CHAN

We find ourselves in the twentieth century, a time when new ways of thinking are ushering in momentous changes that leave all of humanity in a constant state of astonishment. Some people madly rush to embrace them, while others lament and reject them. In either case, there are many who find themselves unable to adapt to their environment so that they are at ease with themselves and can pass the time peacefully. I, of course, am not any different, having gone through periods of embracing these changes and turning against them. However, in the end, I have come to feel that neither of these two options makes sense to me personally. Even after having spent a decade arduously searching for the truth, I still felt like I was lost in a thick fog. However, for the last two years, my thoughts seem to have gravitated toward ideas found in Confucian texts such as "The human mind is precarious. The moral mind is subtle. Have absolute refinement and singleness of purpose. Hold fast to the mean";[1] and "Seek the lost mind,"[2] and "Nourish the flood-like *qi*."[3] When it came to Buddhism, I found persuasive the statement "Establish the universal mind as the central principle; the myriad dharmas are like a mirror's (reflections)."[4] After studying and comparing these three different approaches, I concluded that the first two relied too much on conceptual understanding and hypothetical propositions, and only the last one emerges purely from a realm of self-realizing divine knowledge, with a transcendent universality that encompasses all phenomena. For this reason, I decided to try to study the principles of Chan Buddhism.

Given my ignorance and limited knowledge, how would I be able to find, in today's China, a teacher of great insight and great realization with whom to study? Even if I were to search high and low and circle the globe, I was afraid that there were very few such teachers to be found. I decided, therefore, that the best thing to do would be to retire behind closed doors to study and practice on my own. As for the best place to practice Chan, naturally, the top of a lonely mountain peak or at the far edge of the sea would have been ideal. However, in these times, there are robbers and bandits everywhere, and I would feel uneasy even if I were in a deep mountain and secluded valley or on a desert island in a remote corner of the sea. However, the noise and commotion of a bustling city would also not be conducive for someone just starting to practice. The best thing would be to find something like an urban forest, where I could reside half in retirement and half in seclusion, half cultivating the land and half practicing Chan. Since I would be engaged in farming, I would be able to solve the problem of food and clothing. As for practicing Chan, I would work on refining my character; and if I were to withdraw from public life and live in seclusion, then people would not be envious of me, and I would be able to live a life of stress-free leisure.

1. *The Setting of the Farm-Forest*

The "Scholarly Cases of Lake Ci," chapter 74 of the *Scholarly Cases of the Song and Yuan*, states,

> Yang Jian, courtesy name Jingzhong, was a native of Cixi. He passed the imperial examinations in the fifth year of the Qiandao era (1162), after which he was appointed chief clerk of Fuyang. He would often engage in deep reflection, and so came to realize that the ten thousand things of heaven and earth were all interconnected as one, and that there was nothing outside of the mind. Lu Xiangshan was visiting Fuyang, and at an evening gathering at the Shuangming Pavilion, made frequent mention of "original mind." When Yang Jian asked, "What is this original mind?" Xiangshan replied, "In the dispute that you heard today, one side must have been right and the other wrong. That which discerns which side is right and which is wrong, and decides that A is right and B is wrong: Is that no other than the original mind?"

When he heard this, Yang Jian felt his mind suddenly become lucid and clear and immediately asked, "Is that really all it is?" Sternly, Xiangshan replied, "What else could it be!" Yang Jian then withdrew and, after sitting in meditation the entire night, at daybreak went to see Xiangshan to pay his respects and acknowledge him as his teacher. Later, while on an official trip, he spent the night in the mountains. As he was reading, he came across a passage that he found difficult to understand and which kept him awake all night. Then, just as dawn was about to break, he felt as if something had been dropped off, and his mind became even clearer. In the first year of the Chunxi era (1174), after the death of his mother, he took a leave of absence from his official post.

At one point, concerned that his daily interactions were still not going smoothly, he sat in deep contemplation for several days. Suddenly he hit upon something, and for the first time fully understood the essence of change with its myriad of interconnected transformations, after which his

> mind became clear and serene. He retired with the titled ranks of Academician of Baomo Pavilion, Baron of Cixi County, and Superior Grand Master of the Palace. He passed away in the second year of the Baoqing era (1226) at the age of eighty-six and was posthumously given the epithet Wenyuan, "the Cultured and Profound." He had built a residence in a secluded place on Lake Derun, which he renamed Lake Ci, and even women and children came to know about the person called "Master of Lake Ci." [5]

My Gaya Farm-Forest is located just on the northern corner of Lake Ci. This lake measures only about a mile around its perimeter and is surrounded on three sides by hilltops high and low covered with glistening green vegetation, with a thoroughfare leading to the town on the other. A long causeway runs through the middle of the lake, along the banks of which have been planted scholar trees and poplars that gently sway in the breeze. There is also an arched bridge, in front of which stands a tall pavilion called "Learning from the Past," said to have been built by the Master of Lake Ci. Here are two poems that I wrote to commemorate him.

He carried on the teachings
of Lu Zijing,
A Chan master on the inside
outside a Confucian.
Long, long ago—six centuries
and even more,
This venerable sage of Lake Ci
realized "no-self." [6]

Despite the flow of time,
we share a similar mind:
"Learning from the Past"
has a deep significance!
Up above the hills, the moon
in the cloudless sky
Shone on his wooden clogs
as he neared Lake Ci.[7]

I have also written two poems describing the scenery.

Sweet grasses touch the sky—
  hazy blur of green:
Lake Ci in the early spring
  looks just like a painting.
Pausing at the top of the bridge,
  a breeze fills my sleeves;
In the shade of the green willow,
  I listen to the cooing doves.[8]

The trickling sound of the spring
  like a zither being strummed;
The heady fragrance of flowers
  permeates my simple robes.
A silver coin of mountain moon
  having piqued my interest,
With bamboo pole I set out alone
  to climb the cloudy hills.

2. *My Fields and Gardens*

My plot of land is only about eight or nine mu in size: My two women workers and I are the only ones working it. Apart from the time spent in study and meditation, on the average I need to spend about two hours of work each day on the land. Right now, everyone is using new methods to test the soil quality and select seeds. However, I am unable to purchase chemical fertilizer and modern tools because I have limited financial means. In any case, my idea is to make use of handmade tools even if they are cumbersome, like Gandhi with his spinning wheel. It would also be more appropriate, since not buying things imported from abroad would be a patriotic act of passive resistance.[9]

In the garden there were already some fruit trees such as apricot, green plum, pear, persimmon, pomegranate, peach, and apple. There were also two stands of bamboo that in the spring produced a lot of bamboo shoots, which we would often pack up in jars to give away to friends and relatives. Running through the middle of the garden there is a ditch, in which at times leap quite lively fish and shrimp. The garden is also graced with some weeping willows, as well as scattered clumps of orange osmanthus, dark-green freesia, plum, chrysanthemum, and Chinese parasol trees that are interspersed around the edges. On moonlit nights and flower-filled mornings, it is truly pleasant and lovely. I wrote the following verses about planting mulberry and hemp, gathering lotus leaves, picking tea, planting bamboo, and cultivating apricots, as well as weeding and harvesting greens.

> The pines and chrysanthemums from before
>   entice me to take refuge here;
> The mulberry and hemp I've planted all around
>   illustrate my "family style."
> Living in the forest doesn't necessarily mean
>   there's no work to be done:
> Carrying water, I irrigate the gardens
>   in the light of the setting sun.[10]

> Gentle breezes occasionally stir
>   the stillness of the lotus flowers;
> Light rains regularly add freshness
>   to the tender vegetable shoots.
> The new coolness of this night
>   affords a particular delight;
> As with a hoe in the moonlight
>   I cut through the chilly mist.

I've spent a lot of my time
 scrabbling in the dust,
But lately I've come to learn
 about the farming life.
On this morning in late April,
 so pleasant and so fine,
I accompany the neighbor girls
 going to pick tea.[11]

Along the wall, the soybean vines
 are beginning to ramble;
Around my rooms, the peach trees
 are just starting to bloom.
All night there's been wind and rain
 and the days are still cool;
In front of the stairs, the peony buds
 are just beginning to unfurl.

After having spent my time
    wandering the world,
This little thatched cottage
    I'll happily call home.
This morning's rain shower
    has added to the greens;
Tomorrow I'll take my hoe
    and plant apricot trees.

In the morning, I hoe the fields
    dampened by the dew;
In the evening, I harvest greens,
    smudged by wet soil.
Happily having eaten my fill
    I've nothing more to do,
But sit under the tangerine tree
    listening to the orioles sing.

3. Growing Food and Making Clothes

Apart from the grain and cloth that sometimes we are unable to cultivate or weave, everything we eat and everything we wear we produce ourselves. Even when sometimes the fruit and green vegetables shrivel up due to a lack of rain, instead of going out to buy them, we just eat the dried fruits and vegetables that we had stored away earlier. And whenever we have a bumper crop, we take the surplus to the market and barter it for salt and oil. I have written two poems about this.

> Red rice and green vegetables
>   as sweet as malt sugar;
> White apron and dark clothes
>   both suitably simple.
> Bamboo bowl and gourd cup
>   afford bowl and cup joy:
> Don't blame Yan Hui
>   for bucking the tide![12]

Shu beans like tawny clouds
    boiled with green daylilies;
Wu salt as white as snow
    sprinkled over blue plums.
A newly tailored short blouse
    made of ramie cloth;
Simply made and well-suited
    for a nonworldly life. [13]

4. Visits from Family and Friends

The many visitors I have generally fall into two categories. The first are those who happen to be sightseeing at Lake Ci and stop by to pay a visit in passing. The second category is made up of those who come to discuss more scholarly matters with me. However, being a rather plain and honest person, I don't know how to socialize with them. Whether they belong to the Nine Schools or the Three Teachings, I treat them all in the same sincere way.[14] But they do not take offense at this—in fact, they stick around the entire day, reluctant to go home. I've described this situation like this:

Why take the long journey
    To go to the market,
The southern garden is lush,
    filled with fine fruit.
The northern beds are verdant,
    with vegetables aplenty—
For guests there will be platters
    piled up high!

———

Because I feel for the fallen blossoms
I make sure to sweep the ground;
And I love looking at drifts of snow,
which is why I've planted pines.
Somebody once asked me a question
about life's ultimate meaning:
Flowing streams and floating clouds:
face them both with a smile. [15]

A courtyard of orioles and flowers
who assumed the role of hosts;
Two lakes of breeze and moonlight
who've become good neighbors.
My guests come here to sit together
without uttering a word,
So as to brush away the new dust
that has settled on the path.[16]

There is one thing that I feel bad about when it comes to guests, however. There are times when I want to engage in serious thought, am studying a book describing a system, or am just feeling physically exhausted. I will then lock my doors and refuse to see any visitors. They all forgive me, however, and quietly go away. And now and then, some of the neighborhood children will come looking for me to play with them, only to find that I am unavailable—often when I have some free time or after meals, I enjoy playing with the children, as well as with my cats and my dog—so they will go away in a huff. I worry that they'll never come back. But wouldn't you know it, after a few days, they return; and if unfortunately this time they find me, we all get along even better than before! There are two little poems I have written about this as well.

Quiet and peaceful behind Chan gates—
  an untonsured monastic;
With a mind as cool and composed
  as ice in a pitcher of jade.
I dread hearing the tap on the door
  that will disturb my peace:
It is harder to turn away visitors
  than to rebuff the magistrate![17]

With meditation board and mat,
  I'm just like an old monastic.
When it comes to worldly ways
  I am totally inept!
Although my wicker gate
  is usually kept closed,
There are times it is opened
  for friends from afar.[18]

There are also some young [female] devotees who, wanting to learn more about Buddhism, write to ask if they can come visit me in person. It's not that I am unwilling to help them. It is just that I don't have enough room to put them up or enough food to feed them. But what truly saddened me was that right here in Jiangsu and Zhejiang, provinces known for being rich and prosperous, every year there are many wealthy ladies who fork out money for elaborate Water and Land repentance rituals.[19] They think nothing of spending enormous amounts of money on these but couldn't care in the slightest when it comes to these young people determined to study Buddhism. Once I went to beg for money on these young women's behalf, but those wealthy ladies just scoffed at me saying, "If they want to recite the name of Amitabha Buddha, what need is there for them to learn how to read? And if they want to learn how to read, what need is there for them to recite the name of Amitabha Buddha?"[20] While this view makes no sense at all, there was no arguing with them, and there was nothing more I could say to convince them. If they just spent a little less on extravagant funerals, there would be enough money to run a Buddhist academy![21] For this reason, and with a heavy heart, I wrote the following verses.

The karmic ties between us
must be deep indeed
For you to travel so very far
to visit a kindred spirit.
I hope that you are willing
to keep an open mind:
Raw iron not yet become
highly refined gold.

Bluebirds come carrying
  hundreds of letters
Eagerly wanting to know
  how things are going.
I regret not having learned
  to turn lead into gold
And have a huge mansion
  where guests can stay.[22]

There are so many students
  who are to be pitied:
That they have to go begging
  when they are young.
Why are millions of dollars
  uselessly thrown away,
Converted into paper money
  floating up in the sky?

With tattered monastic robes
completely soaked with tears,
Hastening from east to west
in search of the Dharma.
That these nuns lack education
should fill us with shame:
Will no one open up to them
the gate of nonduality?[23]

5. My Modest Living Quarters

My house is a one-story building of twelve bays. Two of these serve as living quarters for the workers, as well as for storing farming implements; four are used as a bedroom and guest hall; three are designated for meditation room and study; and two are for the kitchen and a wood storage area. Inside the house, there are some casually arranged beds, tables, desks, chairs, Buddhist statues, and bookcases. In the yard, there is a bean arbor and a flower railing, and on either end we planted masses of assorted flowers. In the front, there is a square pond, the water of which is crystal clear and filled with hundreds of little fish swimming about. In short, the decor is so basic and so plain that if in their enthusiasm a distinguished guest were to stay here, they would be plotting their escape within an hour or two! Here are my poems about this.

One whisk, one robe,
  one great big hat;
One lamp, one couch,
  one meditation mat.
One heart, one mind,
  indulging in Chan joy.
One bowl of rice, one of gruel:
  delighting in simple fare!

Because this life is but a dream
    I've chosen to dwell alone;
Building a cottage near Lake Ci
    facing the north embankment.
Its blue waters sink into the void,
    swallowing the myriad forms:
Mind's radiance is as luminous
    as the moon when it is full.

The withered flowers sway,
    resentful of the east wind;
Patches of ash-gray moss
    cling to the fallen reds.
Butterflies love the fragrance
    and are reluctant to go;
Fluttering they still dance
    east of the whitewashed wall.

The rain has newly added
to the profusion of green:
The cauliflowers snow white,
the wheat flowers sparse.
With the days being so long,
outside few people pass by:
Nobody around except the cat
chasing after butterflies.[24]

In the flower-shadowed courtyard
a little puppy slumbers;
Ten thousand cloudless miles,
blue waters and blue skies.
A single disk of luminous moon
over the cold path:
All of this refreshing coolness
is good for meditation!

6. Sketches of Daily Life

Studying

A screen of flowery fragrance,
 a sultry rainfall of red;
A half couch, vapor from the tea
 puffing up white clouds.
The hall emptied of its guests,
 all is peaceful and still:
Perched by my north window,
 I study my ancient texts.

Strumming the Zither

Flowing rivers, lofty mountains—
 the mind of ancient times:
A tune wafts in the soft breeze
 as I strum on the zither.
Incense smoke curls upward
 into the azure skies;
The calls of mountain birds
 add to the harmony.[25]

Painting Orchids

A handful of orchid flowers
  from a well-off neighbor:
A red vase and a purple basin,
  filled with yellow sand.
Drawing crystalline water
  from the ancient well,
I practice painting the most
  graceful flower of all.[26]

Discussing the *Book of Changes*

Light flurries of jade-white snow—
  in the morning discussing the *Book of Changes*;
Facing each other in the lamplight—
  in the evening talking about Chan.
Ashamed to say, I've no special insight
  into the heart of the teachings:
All you wise folk have gathered in vain
  around the teacher's seat!

Practicing Calligraphy

Several stands of slender bamboo
  alongside the low wall;
A pathway of trailing green ivy
  leading to a mountain hut.
Folding banana leaves for paper
  as delicate as clouds,
Playfully, Orchard Pavilion–style,
  I splash a few inky lines![27]

Making Offerings to the Buddha

Gathering the finest of flowers
  to offer the Dharma King:
I ponder on the relative merits
  of dewy orchids and frosty mums.
How long before I gain admittance
  to the Lotus Pond assembly,
Where I will be given lotus flowers
  smelling sweetly of freedom![28]

Gathering Medicinal Herbs

In the mist-covered peaks
  happily gathering herbs;
A curtain of mist and rain
  playing a game of go:
Who says there's no more
  left for me to do—
Requests arrive by telegram
  to write more poems!

Writing

Why strive and struggle so hard
  to display one's talents?
It's just that I have these debts
  all demanding to be paid!
When my poems and translations
  are finished and done,
The postman will show up again
  at my thatched cottage.

Reading Historical Texts

Why, when reading history,
  bother passing judgment?
Why, when chanting poems,
  mull over improvements?
Splendid halls or humble rooms,
  I live where fate takes me.
Facing everything with "no-mind,"
  I can take it all lightly!

Painting Lotuses

A breeze stirs the round leaves
  exposing their red linings;
A white jade crown of flowers,
  a chamber of jasper green.
Who has cut out swatches
  of the Weaving Maid's brocade?
I raise my ink-soaked brush
  to sketch this autumn scene.[29]

Quiet Walking

Half the city surrounded in green—
  the waters of the lake;
One corner of blue sky divides
  the Xianhou Mountain.
Seated meditation and walking:
  the years are going by:
Stealing from this floating life
  this moment of leisure.[30]

Airing Books

Over ten thousand volumes
  of classics East and West
Stored in my meditation room,
  companions in my retreat.
On a whim I spread them out
  beneath the blazing sun,
Hoping that the fierce heat
  will rid them of silverfish.

Releasing the Oriole

It is only delusion or awakening
   that determines a rise or fall;
The ten thousand things originally
   share a common heart:
Lying in bed, I am startled to hear
   the oriole calling its mate;
Pulling on my clothes, I get up
   to release it from its cage.

Burning Incense

Reading scriptures in the canon
   I keep the incense burning;
Ten mu of uncultivated gardens,
   a bamboo hat and a hoe.
Tea brewing in the clay pot
   and thoughts of poetry:
Wind in the pines, a couch,
   and a returning dream.

Lotus-Viewing

On their fat cheeks droplets
of flowing crimson;
Kingfisher-green pendants
of rippling green.
At dawn, I see every field
is dense with leaves:
A hundred thousand pearls
left on a platter of jade.

Thinking About the Past

In the summer cool of water pavilions
we composed poems together;
In the spring warmth of famous gardens
we gave each other flowers.
Like the poets Zhu and Chen
we edited our hundred verses—
Five years since we first parted,
and I have yet to return.[31]

Resting on My Pillow

In the empty hall, I rest on my pillow
  listening to the sound of cicadas:
Willows swaying in the wind,
  the leaves of the lotus round.
There is a certain subtle feeling
  that all of this inspires:
The universe in all its variety
  is inherently as it is.

7. *The Discipline of Meditation Practice*

By nature, and I'm not sure why this is, besides being committed to seek rebirth in the Pure Land, I have always taken a special delight in Chan meditation. Although I don't know much about the methods of practice, I have everywhere and always reflected on sights and sounds and other things. Sometimes fragmentary phrases or words from the sages and wise men of the past, or some verses from a Chan koan come to mind, and I find myself thinking deeply about them. When faced with circumstances—some difficult, some not—I am often able to break the shackles of ignorance, thereby transforming my ordinary mind into a wise one, and difficulties into sources of peace and goodness. However, my habitual tendencies are deeply ingrained and difficult to change, and I am often "ashamed of the limitations of my mind, such that they are always in effect"[32] and my "meager good roots are like candles in the wind; my residual bad habits, like flowers on brocade"; "The winds of ignorance stir the waters in the ancient well, the fires rekindle the ashes left after the kalpa conflagration."[33]

Ever since I read the discourse records of the great Chan masters such as Gaofeng, Hanshan, Zibo, and Zhongfeng, I have been greatly saddened by the thought that they were human beings just like me, with two eyes and two feet, and yet were able to achieve the supreme awakening; while I, like some stupid beast, pass my days in a muddle, concerned only with filling my belly and getting my sleep![34] Hence, I will strengthen my resolve!

Thirty springs have gone by
  since I entered this world.
At times they've been happy,
  at times filled with rage.
Unless you cut yourself free
  with a sharp sword,
It will be difficult to escape
  the cycle of rebirth.[35]

My words may seem enlightened,
  but my practice is still confused.
My practice and realization poles apart—
  I regret the gap between them!
That we possess an innate spiritual source
  is something I vow to realize.
Why complain of the brambles and thorns,
  the ups and downs of the path!

The sordid experiences of life
    are like heaps of trash;
And everywhere that I look
    is blanketed with dust.
The six senses and four elements
    bring nothing but illness;
But seeing form and hearing sound
    can't be just put aside!

Skillfully advancing or retreating
    is no other than the Way;
Complete and constant awareness
    looks like not-knowing.
Holding tight to a single phrase
    is a difficult thing to do;
Even with open eyes, I continue
    to wallow in ignorance.[36]

It is not that my heart
   is insufficiently virile;
But when thoughts arise,
   I find myself in a muddle.
Sadly, under the bright sun
   and a cloudless sky,
Good and bad, right and wrong
   are not up to me.[37]

In vain a hundred thousand swords
   sharpened and at the ready:
Without the skill to slay dragons,
   there is nothing to be done!
Walls of bronze, ramparts of iron,
   impossible to break through:
Many times I've bowed my head
   with tears streaming down.

I have fully and clearly understood
ending both desire and dislike:
I've not yet donned monastic robes,
but already I'm like a monk.
A wide knowledge of the scriptures
will not be of any use at all
If one cannot find one's way through
the perilous gate of Chan.

Sitting quietly on the cushion,
I investigate this mind:
Thoughts bubble up then subside,
arise and then sink away.
Even though I try my utmost
and exert all my strength,
Habits built up over lifetimes
run very deep indeed!

When it comes to this matter
  one cannot rely on others:
Words turn and twist around,
  confounding the truth.
You have to just take a leap
  deep into the vast sea
And snatch away the pearl
  under the dragon's neck.[38]

Breaking out of the tight blockade
  of ten thousand enemies
With wounds all over the body
  and blood everywhere.
If you can with great urgency
  return to the shining light,
The eight sufferings will boil down
  into the richest cream.[39]

A hundred thousand fierce warriors
  trapped in the middle;
Engaged in a life-and-death fight,
  battling against demons.
With one steed and a single lance
  I've decapitated the enemy,
And can now finally return home
  to my father and mother![40]

The above poems describe my experiences practicing Chan by struggling with the huatou. However, the work of navigating against such headwinds was truly difficult and almost unbearable. At one point, when I happened to experience two extremely painful life events, I resolutely took up the huatou and engaged in a life-and-death struggle with the demons of the mind. Although I ultimately emerged victorious, the exhaustion caused by the effort along with the hot weather resulted in my falling ill for a time. After this, I gradually shifted away from this sort of radical practice and adopted a more nurturing and gradual form of cultivation.

8. The Pleasures of Reading Scriptures

Feeding on pine nuts when hungry,
  clothed in green lotus leaves;
I apply myself to the assiduous study
  of the four-chaptered *Lankavatara*.
Is there anyone who sympathizes
  with my earnest aspiration?
Am I not doing it for others,
  as well as for the Buddha?[41]

Right now: Emptiness, Provisional,
  and the Center;
I've familiarized myself with Tiantai's
  Calming and Contemplation sutras.
I've come to understand the Buddha's
  truth and ultimate reality
By not focusing on the individual words
  but on the bigger picture.[42]

The venerable Master Taixu taught me how to read the *Discourse on the Stages of Concentration Practice*, the commentaries on the Abhidharma, the *Treatise on the Great Perfection of Wisdom Sutra*, the *Lankavatara Sutra*, and the *Vimalakirti Sutra*. After reading them, I found them all to be very interesting. The one with which I resonated the most was the *Lankavatara Sutra*. I found the *Discourse on the Stages of Concentration Practice* to be overly broad, which often left me unclear on various points. I also dipped into the three major commentaries and the five minor commentaries of the Tiantai school, and finding the language to be clear and explanations flexible, I did not have any difficulty with them.[43] The *Vinaya of the Southern Mountain* and the *Four Agama Sutras* were very easy to understand as well.[44] I also read with keen pleasure works such as the *Collected Works of Master Zibo*, *The Comprehensive Records of Zhongfeng*, and the works of Venerable Master Hanshan. I found them all so engaging I couldn't put them down!

9. Chanting and Worshipping

If you fail to unfasten the bell
   from the neck of the tiger,
Your life will pass in a drunken daze,
   betraying your divine nature!
Yuansongs and Tangpoems—
   I've laid them all aside,
And with incense burning all day
   I read the *Diamond Sutra*.[45]

Harboring doubts about things
   can bring on troubles;
Reading books is pleasurable
   but can also be a curse.
What once seemed to be a cure
   now feels like a sickness:
In the lonely and empty forest,
   I pay homage to the Buddha.

Abandoning their commentaries and subcommentaries, I began focusing exclusively on the chanting of the sutras. In so doing, I could often sweep away the welter of complications and see directly into my Buddha nature. It was just like breaking up a sky full of thick clouds and miasma, which allowed the disk of pure-white moon to appear, inside and out sparkling and translucent, and at its center still and profound. Over time, without being aware of it, the body and the environment merge, the sound of the chanting would meld together, the eyes and the words merge, thought and scripture totally interconnected and interfused. It was like entering a different realm!

The texts that I used for chanting and practice include: the *Chapter on Knowing Reality*,[46] the *Lankavatara Sutra*, the *Sutra of Perfect Enlightenment*, the *Surangama Sutra*, the *Lotus Sutra*, and the *Diamond Sutra*. As I was living in seclusion with no teachers or friends to turn to for advice and guidance, I sometimes found myself filled with fear and anxiety over falling behind. When this happened, I would rise at midnight, and regardless of whether it was searing cold or blazing hot, pay homage to my root teacher, the Sakyamuni Buddha, and by reverentially taking refuge, I would find my feeble spirit strengthened.

10. *Changes in Meditative States*

Moonlit flowers cast shadows
along the eastern wall—
Meditating in the empty hall
I enjoy the evening cool.
A gust of wind passes by,
chilling to the bone;
In the stillness, the *udambara*
releases its fragrance.[47]

In the empty hall resting on my pillow
I listen to the sound of cicadas,
A breeze blows through the willows,
the lotus leaves are round.
In all this there is a subtle fragrance,
offered for our appreciation:
The myriad phenomena of the world
are inherently what they are.

Since youth, I've worked hard,
  and traveled to distant places;
But after all these years of worry
  I'm no longer so naïve.
Now I have found my way
  into Chan meditation,
Painstakingly brushing away
  every last bit of dust.

When spring comes, all my nights
  are taken up with meditation,
I want to settle this wild mind,
  but so far without success!
The dust built up over lifetimes
  is not easily gotten rid of:
Fully awake and completely alert,
  I sit alone on my rope bed.

It's been a while since any ripples
have stirred the well waters;
At ease, I take delight in listening
to the sound of the bell;
At times there is a certain calm
deep inside the breast;
The moon over the river's heart
shines especially bright.[48]

Now and again, I read
books of immortality;
Day after day, I listen
to the ancient zither.
The moon sets, the stars scatter,
freely coming and going:
Flowers flutter, bangles jangle,
carefree and unconcerned.[49]

From the changing of the seasons
    I understand birth and decay;
And my ten mu of misty waves
    offer a water contemplation.
When let out, it can embrace
    the entire universe;
And when taken in, concealed
    on the tip of a hair.[50]

The lake's brilliance reveals all,
    like a great round mirror;
The mountain's colors display
    the Dharma's pure body.
A completely new scene
    unfolds in the heavens;
How many fully grasp it,
    yield to its intimacy?

How to reduce to nothing
three thousand eons
When a single day has only
twenty-four hours?
I dread the arrival of guests
with their idle chatter,
Stirring up thought-waves,
indulging in silliness.[51]

Ruthlessly, I prune the mind
of idle leaves and branches;
Painful, I cut from my breast
rotten brambles and thorns.
When will I have hacked away
their intertwined roots
So that I can joyfully ascend
the highest peak of all?

Once understood, the horse of the will
    returns to the cave of reason,
And the monkey mind will no longer
    disturb the budding heart.
By scraping and polishing away,
    the brilliance is restored:
Activity and repose alternating
    like the notes of a song.[52]

Ninety days sitting facing the wall
    preserving my path;
Two months of walking meditation,
    knowing this mind:
All the winds of the earth
    can blow as they will;
And wild surging waves
    can freely rise and fall.

Thirty years of grudges and gratitude
    finally come to an end;
Gone in an instant, turned into joy
    like ice melting away.
The double siege has been broken,
    all the enemies defeated.
Now free and completely at ease
    I roam without a care.[53]

I came to the profound realization that the essence of Chan is the wondrous mind of awakening, which is inherent in everyone and readily available to anyone without having to seek it from others. Why, then, should one exert so much effort seeking it, going without sleep and forgetting to eat? It is possible to gradually awaken to the flow of consciousness in the midst of current activities, not forgetting the practice but not forcing either.[54] If one just keeps moving ahead, regardless of the passage of time, your practice will naturally bear fruit, and when conditions are right, success will follow. Be that as it may, I am just a beginner, and I am unsure how to practice in a way that achieves twice the result with half the effort, without falling into the demonic path. All I can do is select a good method that is efficient and will lead to better results without falling into delusion. For now, I will follow the methods of meditation taught by Master Hanshan, whom I have always respected, and see what things look like after a few years! His guidelines are as follows:

1. You must see through all the worldly realms and not follow that which is turned about by deluded conditioning.

2. You must realize that this is a great matter of life and death. Resolve to have a heart as firm as a stone and do not allow your aspiration to be overpowered by deluded ideas and external conditions.

3. You must recognize all your past habitual vices and wash them all away without leaving a trace.

4. You must really give up your life. Do not be hindered by death and rebirth, illness and calamity, or bad karma.

5. You must have right faith and right views. You cannot listen to the fallacies of heterodox teachers.

6. You must recognize the true intentions of the ancients. Investigate and practice huatou.

7. Remain mindful in all daily activities and wherever you are. Do not be confused by illusions. There should be no space between thoughts, with movement and stillness as one.

8. You must keep your sincere thoughts moving forward. You cannot wait for your mind to attain enlightenment.

9. You must be in it for the long haul. Even if your aspirations are not as high as those of the ancients, you must not give up. You can never be satisfied with less.

10. When practicing, you must give up and put to rest all thoughts. Give them up, and then give them up again. Put them to rest, and then put them to rest again. When you have given them up until there is nothing more to give up and put them to rest until there is no longer any place where they can rest, there will automatically be good results.[55]

11. *A Lingering Attachment to Poetry*

Alone, legs in the lotus position,
  I sit in the empty hall:
My mind now clear and tranquil,
  all worries forgotten.
There is only the poetry demon
  that still hangs around;
Like threads wrapping around
  my emptied-out guts![56]

Reading scriptures in the canon
  I keep the incense burning;
Ten mu of uncultivated gardens,
  a bamboo hat and a hoe.
Tea brewing in the clay pot
  and thoughts of poetry:
Wind in the pines, a couch,
  and a returning dream.[57]

Suffering hardship in the deep forest,
in order to study the Way,
My aspiration has been to rid myself
of all worldly delusions.
Ashamed to say, I've found it hard
to eradicate all old habits:
In just a single night I've recited
thirty different poems!

Twisting and winding:
the narrow path;
Rickety and sparse:
the bamboo fence.
Peacefully on my pillow,
I take a noon nap;
In the deep forest at dusk
I sit writing poems!

After months on the meditation mat
swallowing spiky chestnuts,
I steal a bit of leisure to revisit
one of my old pursuits;
A hundred fresh new poems—
how difficult it really is!
What I'll leave in the world
are tracks on the snow![58]

Dongpo [Su Shi] said, "When composing poems, you must be exceedingly quick, as if seeking enlightenment, for once a pure scene is lost, it becomes difficult to chase it down again." Duling [Du Fu] said, "As you get older, the rhythm of poetry becomes more and more refined." And there are the lines by Venerable Qichan [Jichan]: "My temple hairs fall out one by one, / and lines word by word become difficult to write." [59] These are all descriptions of a person's mental state when writing poetry. It is also as Jiannan said: "How will my writings ever startle the world? / In vain I squander my efforts as poet!"[60] These all describe the frustration and the futility of writing poetry. Then there are great Chan masters such as Zhongfeng [Mingben], Zibo [Zhenke], and Jiyin, who all wrote gathas proscribing poetry.[61] Nevertheless, every time I engage in the "samadhi of play," out comes a continuous stream of unimaginably beautiful words![62]

It has always been the case that a third of my poems bear no resemblance to prose and two-thirds bear no resemblance to poetry and should be just regarded as folksy tunes! Ever since I started learning about Buddhism, however, I have focused on getting rid of my bad habits and inclinations. One by one, I've been able to gradually eliminate habits related to being arrogant, resentful, narrow-minded, short-tempered, stubborn, and tempestuous, along with such things as fancy clothes, tasty food, going to bed and getting up late, and striving for fame and wealth. However, I still have some real difficulties when it comes to poetry.

> Rouge and powder have ceded
>   to the simple and plain;
> Obsessed with smoke and mist
>   I don't care for flattery.
> And yet, for no apparent reason,
>   I find my feelings stirred
> When swallows come flying in,
>   speaking of old loves.

Last winter, when I was practicing the Lotus Samadhi ritual, I forced myself to lay down my writing brush for half a year.[63] To my surprise, I felt tranquil and at ease. However, and I don't know why it is, now I feel everything bubbling up with great force inside of me, and I find it impossible not to move when I feel so impelled, and impossible to stop when I feel the need to do so. There is one thing that I can console myself with, however: Although I write when I feel inspired to do so, immediately after having written something, I put it aside without thinking about it anymore. And I don't worry in the slightest about whether the wording is skillful or clumsy, or the parallelism is smooth and regular. All I try to do is shed some light on the truth; I have no desire to be showy or flamboyant.

A former student showed up one day wanting me to write some poems especially for his little magazine. However, when he saw the drafts of the poems, he said, "No one wants to read this sort of poem. Please write us something different." Laughing, I replied, "Don't you remember the lines from Lu You's poem: 'Only if it is not swayed by external things can something be called learning; / Only if it is loved by the common people can it be considered poetry'?[64] And Letian [Bai Juyi] who said, 'The common people only like my *Song of Everlasting Sorrow* and my *Ballad of the Lute*, but where in these works can you find my true identity?'" Hearing this, my visitor just stared at me blankly, then, after accusing me of just being unwilling to write him some more beautiful poems, he left in a huff.

12. My Aspirations

I once had a visit from a woman friend who enjoyed quite a reputation in the world and whom I had not seen for a long time. Worried that I was falling out of step with the times by staying home and not wanting to go out in society, she was determined to drag me away from my mountain and get me involved in something or other. I told her that there was no need to worry about me, as I had already been through quite enough. I then composed this poem on the spot and gave it to her to read.

> When first I settled in the forest
>   in order to study the Way,
> Kith and kin in countless ways
>   pitied me for my plight.
> Habits built up over lifetimes
>   are not easily changed:
> Three letters of resignation
>   in just a single day!

She read this poem but said nothing. Then she went on to ask me, "Are you assuming this haughty and aloof attitude because you aspire to a position in the literary world like that of Mojie and his Wangchuan Estate,[65] Zimei and his Thatched Cottage,[66] or Letian's Thatched Cottage on Mount Lu?[67] Or are you imitating Master Shaoyong's 'Nest of Tranquility and Joy'[68] or Tao Yuanming's 'House of the Five Willows'?[69] Or are you modeling yourself on Mahasattva Fu living on Mount Song[70] or Liu Yiming (352–410) of the Mount Lu Lotus Society?"[71] I replied to her questions with the following eight poems.

The waters of Lake Ci by my door
  are pure and refreshing;
Mountain peaks surround my home
  with jagged emerald hues.
I am relying on the numinous power
  of their springs and stones
To wash away the muddle and dust
  of all I've been through.

In the depths of white clouds
  a three-room dwelling,
In the shade of green trees
  a ten-mu garden.
This seclusion came about
  completely naturally,
Not from hating the world
  or escaping into Chan.

Blossoming flowers bring joy,
  and fading ones sorrow:
But joy and sorrow are states
  we bring upon ourselves.
All you need is for the mind
  to be completely at ease,
To enjoy spring and autumn
  with neither sorrow nor joy.

In the hurly-burly of the world,
  who knows themselves?
A retreat with woods and springs
  and gulls as companions,
Teaching and cultivating myself,
  I keep up my own spirits;
No matter if people call me this
or if they call me that.[72]

Iron clappers and bronze lutes
  sound a northern tune,
Silver flutes and jade reeds
  play a southern lyric.
Now on nights of autumn moon
  and of spring breezes,
I listen quietly to the pine waves
  rising from all around.

Human feelings are as thin
as billowing autumn clouds,
Worldly affairs are as thick
as surging river waters.
I rely on intensive meditation
to counteract all of these:
Otherwise, what can be done
to ease a thousand cares?[73]

Leaving everything, I've returned
to Master Bodhidharma:
Nine years of facing the wall,
with a single aspiration.
Holding fast to the sharp sword,
wrapped in spring breeze,
Undaunted by all the demons
appearing before him![74]

In a dream, the yellow millet cooks
in the blink of an eye,
A thousand sorrows, ten thousand grudges
completely whittled away.
How many years have been squandered
shedding tears of heartbreak—
And, carefully counting them all up,
quite a few jokes as well.[75]

To sum up, I am neither a poet nor a Chan master hoping to enjoy a bit of future fame. But neither have I idly wasted my time, content to sit back and enjoy life while eating up my parents' inheritance and being a burden to my family. I follow the principle of "a day without work is a day without food," and I work hard on my farm to earn my livelihood. At the same time, I pursue my own interests, practicing Chan methods for my own benefit, and always reading Buddhist scriptures and other kinds of books. If someone comes to me with questions, I will without any hesitations share what I truly know without making it difficult. I love my country, and I am also faithful to my Buddhist convictions, daily reciting the *Yogacara Bodhisattva Precepts*[76] and the *Chapter on Knowing Reality*.[77] I am happy to serve society wherever I can be of help. As for matters relating to Buddhism that need to be promoted, I am certainly willing to contribute as much as possible, if it does not arouse people's envy. As for the Buddhist teachings that I have been studying, I have decided to follow the words of Chan Master Yunju Hongjue [Caodong Master Yunju Daoying]: "Desire less and be content. Do not covet worldly glory. Endure hunger and thirst. Aspire to nonaction. Find fulfillment in the Buddha's teachings. In life, there are nine deaths for every birth. Do not cast yourself aside. In life and death, do not go against the Buddha's teachings. Be resolute and unwavering. Do not betray the Tathagata."[78] Persist to the end. However, now everything is [still] in an experimental stage, and I would greatly welcome criticisms and suggestions from both farmers and Buddhist scholars everywhere.

PART TWO

More Poems on a Life of Seclusion

MISCELLANEOUS VERSES ON GAYA

1

In this life, rare pleasures
  are found in leisure:
Ten mu of woods and gardens
  in a mountain corner.
Cold beds full of vegetables,
  a pond full of water:
Though there's a wicker gate
  it's usually kept closed.[1]

2

Relationships bring people
 the greatest suffering;
Money is valued far more
 than righteousness.
Looking again, there's only
 the moon in the pines—
A slice of pure radiance
 shining through time.

3

A simple and modest lifestyle
 brings tranquility and joy:
A low fence, a humble home
 in which to live in peace.
This body will happily grow old
 among these woods and springs:
Making up for a lifetime of books
 I have not yet read!

4

Blue cypress and green pine
    are models of integrity,
Clear clouds and bright moon
    convey a Chan heart.
The life that I live nowadays,
    few can appreciate:
On a bamboo couch and mat,
    sitting deep into the night.

5

Seeking nothing from the world,
    my heart is ever joyful;
Unperturbed by poverty or pain,
    I trust in my karma.
At dawn sitting cross-legged
    on top of a boulder—
A transparently clear spirit
    is a heaven of its own.

6

Hidden among forest and springs,
    the myriad worries cease;
Let other people call me this
    or then again, that.
In the turbulent secular world,
    intimate friends are rare:
Along the shore, a clear breeze
    and bright moon wander.

7

A quiet and winding path
    pale with yellow flowers;
A tranquil and placid lake
    quiet with white swans.
If you see with perfect clarity
    and direct awareness
Why, may I ask, go knocking
    on the gates of Chan?[2]

8

Don't talk of meditative insight
into both past and present:
Ingrained habits keep acting up,
like my love of poetry!
This fragment of idle feelings
has nowhere to settle:
Flowers blossom, flowers wither:
and I will always care!

9

A scattering of willows by the pond,
fish startled from their dreams;
Masses of flowers beyond the fence,
birds that shatter one's heart.
If fish and birds were able to show
the actual emptiness of form;
You wouldn't need a snap of fingers
to enter the Profound Gate![3]

10

In the morning light, butterflies
   emerge in swarms;
In the evening glow, crows
   return to roost.
A word to those on the road
   seeking wealth and fame:
Why not enjoy a little leisure
   here beneath the trees?

11

Do not speak of the world
   and its endless affairs,
Let's play a game of go
   here among the trees.
On a bamboo cot by the flowers
   napping in the green shade,
By the clear lake's rocky banks
   enjoying the clear ripples.

12

The wild mind has been slowly tamed—
what more is there to seek?
The antelope is hanging by its horns,
everything is now serene.
On the lake at midnight
playing a jade flute;
By the shore in early summer
wearing a light coat.[4]

13

Gathering wild greens
for a visitor's meal;
Picking mountain flowers
for a bronze bowl:
Everything I see before me
full of natural charm—
Picking here, gathering there:
as happy as can be!

14

Straw sandals and bamboo staff,
  I am a person of leisure;
Walking alone in a thousand peaks,
  untainted by worldly dust.
Heading home at the end of day
  I look out by the bridge:
As the head of a duck pokes through
  the lake full of spring!

15

This matter is perfectly obvious
  but also fully concealed:
Why then spend every day
  in frantic pursuit?
Right there in front of you
  is the Buddha-body:
No practice, no realization:
  ever still and luminous.

16

In a broken-legged pot
  cooking taro on the fire;
With a blunt-edged hoe
  splitting open the sky:
Who is the host, who the guest,
  who the essence-function?
There is no self and no other,
  no East and no West.[5]

17

As absolute and relative dissolve,
  the mind is slowly stabilized;
Moving according to conditions:
  nothing supernatural about it!
Hiding talents, covering traces
  deep under the forest trees;
Laughing at this floating world
  between being and nothingness.[6]

18

A single steed: Zhuang Zhou
makes all things equal.
The "three mysteries": Linji
sings his teaching style.
Looking at them more closely,
they are child's play!
The ascetic bent over laughing
is the Elder of Gaya![7]

19

Having left the bustling city,
my mind in a muddle,
I headed straight to the cliff
from where to let go.
A vast expanse of clear sky,
a bright crescent moon:
This layperson from Gaya
is full of carefree joy![8]

20

A bodhisattva's deep compassion
    is difficult to emulate!
The emptiness of the two schools:
    it is hard to reconcile.
Upon reflection, it is better to be
    an ordinary know-nothing:
Planting bamboo, sowing flowers,
    playing the zither every day![9]

21

I don't care about my writings
    lasting a thousand autumns;
Nor do I wish for achievements
    celebrated for all eternity.
But there is a leisurely feeling
    that I cannot do without:
Every day all through spring
    kept busy by my flowers!

22

Poetic lines usually emerge
from within dreams,
Worldly sentiments are slowly
forgotten in meditation.
The unhurried life gives rise
to a special awareness:
Flowers bloom by the hedge
after a night of frost.

23

Rising in the middle of the night
I sit and burn incense,
Quietly facing the censer smoke,
worldly matters forgotten.
A solitary radiance shines clear
without any obstructions:
One would think it was the moon
shining in a cloudless sky.

24

The daytime hours now go by
passed in leisure,
Thirty years of old grievances
quietly fade away.
The blazing fire of true emptiness
burns in the furnace;
The eighty-thousand afflictions
drifting like snow.

25

All things have from the start
formed a single body:
Greedy for life, fearful of death,
wanting to be secure.
You must earnestly remind
the neighbor's children
Not to go angling in the pond
for the five-colored fish.[10]

26

The self-nature of Amitabha
natural from the start;
With just one single phrase
all the dharmas complete.
Gathering in the six senses,
continual pure thoughts:
Sound after sound penetrating
the innermost perfection.[11]

27

After a day spent in chitchat,
I regret the wasted time;
Last night the autumn winds
snapped the green lotus.
Regretting I have no remedies,
I turn away my visitors;
To ponder behind closed doors
the illness of Vimalakirti.[12]

28

Vowing a heart as constant
as the sun and moon,
I don't want my name
left behind in the world.
Next year, I'll go to a place
deep in the mountains:
Clouds skimming the ground,
books blocking the door.

29

Stubborn and lacking talent,
cast aside by the world:
A modest life at the riverside
is what suits me best:
Autumn winds over a thatched hut:
pulling up vines for patching;
Spring rains in the empty forest:
breaking off willows for cooking.

30

Crystal-clear pond waters
all containing the moon;
Slender flowering branches
blanketed with spring.
Every form I see before me
is the peerless Dharma;
Everywhere with everything
I end up being friends.

31

"Snow, moon, breeze, blossoms"
add to the poetic words;
"Joy, sorrow, parting, reunion"
stir up worldly feelings.
Creating something out of nothing
are legs added to a snake:
Taking such pains to whittle away
and level what's uneven.[13]

32

I've studied the sutras but not yet grasped
the ultimate source of the Dharma,
Only by practicing stillness can one know
it is not easy to become a buddha.
I am ashamed that my mind is clear
but my strength insufficient—
When will I finally begin to be able
to turn back the raging tide?

33

Twisted roots, tangled branches,[14]
a road full of hardships:
So much illness, so much sorrow,
so much dissatisfaction!
Sitting quietly on the cushion,
repenting past deeds:
The night is like cool water,
the moon a silver coin.

THOUGHTS ON INJURING MY HAND WHEN CHOPPING WOOD

1

A sparse fence and a small hut
  at the edge of the lake;
Carrying water and chopping wood,
  are activities I know well.
Cakes made of sesame and bran
  will do to keep me fed;
Barley and cabbage porridge
  get me through the morning.
In years gone by I was a scholar
  with three thousand books,
Today I'm just a poor old woman
  with one bundle of firewood.

If you regard a tiny speck of dust
as equal to a dharma realm,
Why should you seek happiness,
and what need to be sad?

2

Inferior to others in a hundred ways
and mistaken in a thousand;
Finding myself in these dire straits
upon what else can I rely?
Blood relatives all at heaven's edge:
we've long been apart.
Teachers and students at sea's end,
news of them is rare.
Planting bamboo, growing flowers,
my state of mind is tranquil.
Tying vines to patch up my cottage,
my way of life is modest.
Thirty days and only nine meals
is a usual thing for me.
The courtyard is now overgrown,
alone, I close my door.[1]

THOUGHTS ON LIVING IN THE FOREST

1

The great Dharma has long been in decline,
  who is there to pass on the Buddha's Way?
Silent and lonely, a teaching for the ages,
  quiet and still, the glow of a single lamp.
By dropping away, the subtleties are seen,
  "self" and "other" suddenly transcended.
The unspoken is louder than a thunderclap:
  across the four seas, looking for a ceasefire.[1]

2

Having grown weary of the muddled world,
 I entered the mountains ambitions unfulfilled.
In years gone by, I was tied down by duties,
 but today I go along with the flow of time.
Having joyfully understood the "unborn,"
 occasionally I can ride the boat of prajna.
A bright sliver of moon among the trees,
 together with all things wandering at ease.[2]

RETURNING HOME TO GAYA FOREST, JOYFULLY WRITTEN

A few rooms in this remote forest:
　　even a brief sojourn brings a smile.
Green encircles the Lake Ci waters;
　　blue divides the Mount Fubi slopes.
A meatless meal of brown rice and beans;
　　sitting here I take joy in the quiet leisure.
This secluded spot is perfect for meditating,
　　and soon I will go and close up the gate.[1]

ACKNOWLEDGMENTS

It is a truth universally acknowledged, or should be, that no book comes into being without the encouragement and often considerable assistance of many others. I owe a special debt of gratitude to Professor Wilt L. Idema, who looked over the early versions of this book and made some greatly useful corrections and comments. I would like also to offer a bow of gratitude to Shambhala Publications president Nikko Odiseos, whose enthusiasm for this project overrode his understandable concerns over the feasibility of publishing translations of Chinese poetry. A deep bow as well to Shambhala Publications editor Sami Nicole Ripley, who replied so kindly to my initial inquiries and has been unfailingly responsive and helpful throughout the entire process of readying the manuscript for publication. I am also most grateful to Emily Wichland for her careful and sensitive copyediting and hasten to note that if any errors or infelicities remain, they are my responsibility alone. It is largely thanks to the generous efforts of these four people that a whole new audience may now come to know about this extraordinary early twentieth-century Chinese Buddhist woman.

NOTES

Translator's Introduction

1. The original name, Cixi, was changed in 1959 to Cicheng. A town that traces its history back to the eighth century, it is located fifteen miles northwest of the city of Ningbo and about seventy-five miles south of Shanghai.
2. For an excellent introduction to this revival and its historical context, as well as to Taixu, Yinguang, and other important figures, see Benjamin Brose, ed., *Buddhist Masters of Modern China* (Shambhala, 2025).
3. Lake Ci was originally known by various different names, including Lake Kan after the mountain next to it, but was renamed by Yang Jian.
4. Farm-forest (*nonglin*) is a term now used to translate agro-forestry. In the Buddhist context, it refers to the close relationship between Buddhists, especially Chan monastics, and the practice of agriculture and forestry. There are many historical accounts of Chinese

Buddhist monks who transformed wilderness into cultivated land. Just one example among many is the Chan master Yongjing (fl. eleventh century), who while abbot of Shousheng Monastery in Xiangshan county (near present-day Ningbo) cultivated three hundred *mu* (nearly fifty acres) of farmland and planted more than a hundred thousand trees. See Huang Minzhi, "Buddhist Monasteries and Local Public Welfare Projects in the Song Dynasty" (*Songdai Foxue siyuan yu defang gongyi shiye*), in *Fojiao de Sixiang yu wen hua: Yinshun Zunshi bashi jinliu shouqing lun* [Buddhist thought and culture—collected papers celebrating the 86th birthday of Master Yinshun], ed. Shengyan (Faguang chubanshe, 1991), 271.

5. Gaya city is the location of Bodhgaya, where the Buddha is said to have attained awakening, and nearby Mount Gayashirsha, known today as Brahmayoni, is where he would often preach.
6. Zhang was also a great admirer of Leo Tolstoy, whom she regarded as a Chan master of sorts. In 1934, she published a long article entitled "Tolstoy and Farming-Chan," *Haochao yin* 15, no. 8 (1934): 40–45.
7. For a succinct description of this Chan practice, see Guo Gu's introduction to Master Xuyun, in Brose, ed., *Buddhist Masters of Modern China*, especially pp. 26–27.
8. The Tiantai school emerged in China between the sixth and eleventh centuries as an attempt by great thinkers such as Zhiyi (538–597), regarded as the school's founder, to absorb and integrate the many different and often contradictory Buddhist teachings imported from India. Its dual emphasis on both scriptural study and meditative practice made it attractive to an intellectual such as Zhang.

Verses on Returning to the Land

1. **investigating things**: A term used in the early twentieth century to refer to the Western science of physics, but Zhang may well be referring more generally to the neo-Confucian practice of systematically studying principles in order to reach a personal grasp of the (moral) truth of things.
2. **Adversity and prosperity are unavoidable:** Here Zhang refers to two of the sixty-four hexagrams of the *Book of Changes* (*Yijing*): *pi* symbolizes misfortune, and *tai* symbolizes prosperity. Together, they refer to the inevitable ups and downs of life.

   abstinence brings only pain: A reference to the Daoist practice of abstaining from eating cereals as part of their pursuit of immortality (or, at least, a long life).

   Chang'an: Present-day Xian. Chang'an was the capital of the Tang dynasty (618–907). After the bloody An Lushan rebellion (755–763), the once glorious empire fell into gradual decline.

   Penglai mountain: Penglai is a legendary mountain in Chinese mythology said to be inhabited by immortals.

   Hidden fish are happy in clear waves / Exotic birds choose the greenest trees: *Hidden fish* and *exotic birds* most likely refer to social outliers of integrity and talent.

   Confucius left for the state of Qi: Deeply disillusioned with the unethical behaviors of the ruler of his home state of Lu, in 497 Confucius left with some of his disciples and went to the neighboring state of Qi. His decision to leave reflected his refusal to compromise his principles.

Bodhidharma crossed on a reed: Bodhidharma, traditionally regarded as the first patriarch of Chan, is said to have crossed the Yangzi River on a reed on his way to northern China.

Walking, walking, again walking: This is a famous line from the first of the "Nineteen Old Songs," written anonymously by poets living during the chaotic years that marked the end of the Han dynasty (206–220). This line describes the wandering of a traveler far from home.

3. **Unwilling to grovel for a meager wage:** The Chinese poet Tao Yuanming (c. 365–427) refused to "bow for five pecks of rice"—that is, to compromise his integrity in exchange for a meager salary. Instead, he left his official post and returned to the countryside to live a quiet life as a farmer.

Lotus leaves will be fine for clothes: In "Encountering Sorrow" (*Lisao*), ascribed to the exiled official Qu Yuan (fourth century B.C.E.), the poet declares that he can easily "fashion clothes from lotus leaves."

countryfolk friends: Literally, woodcutters and cowherds.

A Note on Gaya Farm-Forest

1. The scholar-official Feng Yuanyang (1586–1644) was born in Cixi and known for his painting and calligraphy. He was highly valued by the emperor, who was reluctant to accept Feng's request that he be allowed to retire. When he was finally able to do so, he died on his way home in 1644, the year the dynasty itself fell.

2. This site was named after the famous poet-recluse Tao Yuanming (365–427).
3. Mount Kan is north of Cixi, underneath which Zhang's property was located. Lake Ci, the scenic lake at the foot of Mount Kan, was originally a small, shallow natural body of water that was excavated and enlarged in the early eighth century (713–741) for use as a reservoir for irrigation. It is to this day known for its beauty and crystalline waters.
4. Master Yang was the neo-Confucian philosopher who founded a famous academy on the bank of Cihu. Yang Jian himself was known as Master Cihu.
5. Yao Mo (1465–1538) was a famous scholar-official, military leader, and Cixi native. Woman Martyr Jin was the young second wife of a local fisherman who, after her husband's death at sea, patiently endured the abuse of her mother-in-law and defiantly resisted the improper advances of the latter's merchant lover. In 1853, her filial chastity was officially recognized by the imperial court.
6. The opening couplet of a poem by the philosopher-poet Liu Yuxi (772–842). This poem, entitled "An Inscription for My Rustic Hut," describes a life of contentment living in a ramshackle hut, away from the hurly-burly of the world.

Experiments in a Life of Farming-Chan

1. This statement, which first appeared in the *Book of Documents* (*Shangshu*), an ancient collection of rhetorical prose attributed to

ancient sages, has served as the foundation of Chinese political philosophy for over two thousand years. During the Song (960–1279) and Ming (1368–1644) dynasties, neo-Confucian thinkers often wrote about how to deal with the distinction between the moral mind and the human or everyday mind that was often the source of harmful desires.

2. The notion of seeking the lost mind originally comes from the great Confucian thinker Mencius (372–289 B.C.E.). See D. C. Lau, trans., *Mencius* (Penguin Books, 2003), 167.
3. The notion of qi (sometimes translated as "vital force") plays an important role in neo-Confucian philosophical thinking. The general idea is that a person's qi can be very turbid, in which case it makes it impossible to manifest the higher principles of morality. However, this qi can be nourished and clarified by means of personal cultivation and study. By so doing, a person's virtue and goodness may be made manifest. See Lau, trans., *Mencius*, 77–78.
4. This phrase appears in *Zongjing lu* [Records of the Source Mirror], by Yongming Yanshou (904–975), CBETA T48, no. 2016, 417a20–21.
5. *Scholarly Cases of the Song and Yuan* is an intellectual history of the Song (960–1279) and Yuan (1271–1368) dynasties, begun by Huang Zongxi (1610–1695) and later completed by his son and others. It comprises accounts of the lives and teachings of more than twenty-seven hundred scholars, primarily from the various schools of neo-Confucianism.
6. **Lu Zijing**: Lu Jiuyuan's courtesy name.

7. **Learning from the Past:** This refers to the name of a pavilion that stands on the causeway extending from the northern bank to the heart of Lake Ci. It was first built in 1776 and has since been restored.

   wooden clogs: The Buddhist nature poet Xie Lingyun (385–433) invented wooden clogs with removable teeth, which he used for trekking through the mountains.

8. **Lake Ci in the early spring**: Literally, the third month of the lunar calendar, which usually falls in April or May.

   Pausing at the top of the bridge: The curved stone bridge leading to the Learning from the Past Pavilion.

9. In 1905, the Shanghai Chamber of Commerce passed a resolution calling for a boycott of American goods in protest of US immigration policies. Such boycotts continued to be a form of resistance against foreign powers throughout the early twentieth century.

10. **family style**: A term that often refers to the teaching methods or traditions of a particular Buddhist lineage. Here, Zhang may be referring to her stated aims of self-sufficiency.

11. **scrabbling in the dust:** This phrase was often used to refer to the chaos and hardships of an unstable society, especially in official circles.

    farming life: Literally, "planting mulberry and hemp," often used as a general term for farming.

12. Yan Hui (521–481 B.C.E.) was one of the earliest and most beloved disciples of Confucius. In the *Analects* we find Confucius exclaiming,

"The Master said, What a fine man Hui was! One container of rice, one dipperful of drink, living in a back alley—others couldn't have endured the gloom of it, but he never let it affect his happiness. What a fine man Hui was!" Burton Watson, trans., *The Analects of Confucius* (Columbia University Press, 2007), 43.

13. Shu is the traditional name for the area known today as Sichuan, where fermented soybeans, usually made into a paste, are a staple of the cuisine. The salt from Wu (the lower Yangzi area) was regarded as being of the highest quality due to its mild flavor and bright white color. Blue plums served with a sprinkling of this salt are considered a delicacy.
14. The "Three Teachings" refer to Confucianism, Buddhism, and Daoism; the "Nine Schools" refer to the various strains of traditional Chinese religious and philosophic thought.
15. "Life's ultimate meaning" is an allusion to the poem by the Tang poet, artist, and Buddhist layman Wang Wei entitled "Answering Vice-Prefect Zhang," the concluding couplet of which can be translated: "You ask me about ultimate universal principles / The fisherman's song enter deep into the cove."
16. **brush away the new dust:** That is, they sit in meditation in order to clear away the dust of worries and anxieties.
17. A common trope in writings about the recluse is having them be sought out by a high government official who, recognizing their integrity, tries unsuccessfully to lure them back into official service. Here, Zhang finds turning away the children who come knocking at her door to be more difficult!

18. Confucius's *Analects* opens with the lines: "The Master said, Studying, and from time to time going over what you've learned—that's enjoyable, isn't it? To have a friend come from a long way off—that's a pleasure, isn't it?" Watson, trans., *Analects of Confucius*, 16.
19. An elaborate and costly Buddhist ritual requiring the intensive labor of many monks and temple staff.
20. An early feminist, Zhang studied and wrote extensively about the role of women in Buddhism. She was very concerned that they be afforded the possibility to pursue advanced studies in Buddhism and become fully ordained if they so desired. Although China had a tradition of Buddhist nuns and laywomen, many still believed that women's piety should be confined to the home and that they should recite Amitabha's name rather than do any kind of study.
21. An important component of the revival of Buddhism in twentieth-century China was the establishment of Buddhist seminaries for training monastics as well as laypersons. Zhang visited a number of these seminaries, and in the early 1940s would be invited to teach in one that was opened just for female monastics.
22. There is an allusion here to the first two lines of the poem by the great Tang poet Du Fu entitled "Song About My Thatched Hut Destroyed by Autumn Winds": "How can I acquire a great mansion of a thousand rooms / where all the world's poor scholars might gather in joy."
23. **the gate of nonduality**: Referring to the Buddhist path. Although monks had opportunities to pursue their studies at monasteries and Buddhist seminaries, this was not the case for nuns. One exception

was the Wuchang Women's Institute of Buddhist Studies, established by Master Taixu in 1924.

24. **wheat flowers sparse**: That is, the wheat is ripening.
25. There is an indirect allusion here to a famous zither player from ancient China named Bo Ya, whose playing was said to perfectly embody and evoke the natural sounds of waves and forests. His friend Zhong Ziqi was the only one able to hear these sounds in his playing, and when he died, Bo Ya broke his zither because he felt no one else could understand him.
26. **the ancient well**: A reference to the well of the inkstone used in Chinese brush painting.

    graceful flower: The word *danbo*, here translated as "graceful," refers to people or things that are simple and unpretentious with no interest in fame and fortune. It is often applied to orchids, which grow in secluded valleys and, with their elegant blossoms and subtle fragrance, are said to symbolize transcendent and pure beauty.
27. **Folding banana leaves for paper**: The Tang dynasty monk Huaisu (fl. eighth century), famous for his cursive calligraphy, is said to have been so poor that he could not afford to buy paper. He planted banana trees around his dwelling place and used their leaves for practicing.

    Orchid Pavilion–style: In 353, a group of literati met at the Orchid Pavilion on Mount Kuaiji in Zhejiang province to drink, paint, and compose poetry. Among them was the talented calligrapher Wang Xizhi (303–360), who wrote out what would become a text often copied by other calligraphers titled "Preface to the Poems Composed at the Orchid Pavilion" (*Lanting xu*).

28. Rebirth in the Pure Land is believed to take place from a lotus flower, frequently used in Buddhism as a symbol of transcendent purity.
29. **Weaving Maid's brocade**: In Chinese mythology, the star Vega in the constellation Lyra is identified as the Weaving Maiden, one of the seven daughters of the Jade Emperor. Regarded as the goddess of weaving, she is said to have used clouds to weave brocade for her father's royal robes. Used to refer not only to particularly beautiful silk fabric but also to beautifully crafted poetry and painting.
30. **Quiet Walking**: The title of this poem is a term that refers not so much to formal walking meditation practice but rather to quietly and slowly walking around after a long period of meditation in order to keep from getting drowsy.

    Xianhou Mountain: Another name for Mount Fubi.

    leisure: A word that appears often in classical Chinese poetry, especially in poems describing the reclusive life. It is a word with a very deep resonance, one that has recently been eloquently described by the contemporary Korean philosopher Byung-Chul Han in his *Vita Contemplativa: In Praise of Inactivity* (Polity, 2024).
31. **we composed poems together**: The reference here is to the practice of people getting together and writing poems on assigned topics and rhyme schemes.

    Zhu and Chen: Zhu Yizun (1629–1709) and Chen Weisong (1625–1682) were known for their lyric poetry, characterized by an emphasis on the inner emotional worlds and often romantic sentiment. Zhang wrote (and published) many poems of this kind when she was younger.

32. This phrase can be found in a text by the Song dynasty master Juefan Huihong (1107–1128) in his collection entitled *Shimen wenzichan* [Literary Chan from Stone Gate Monastery]. See CBETA J23, no. B135, 660b5–6.

33. I am unable to trace the exact source of the lines in these last two quotes. In the kalpa of destruction, the entire physical universe is said to go up in flames.

34. Here Zhang refers to some of the most eminent post-Tang Chan masters: Gaofeng Yuanmiao (1238–1295); Hanshan Deqing (1546–1623); Zibo Zhenke (1543–1603); and Zhongfeng Mingben (1263–1323).

35. **sharp sword**: The sword of wisdom that cuts through ignorance.

36. **Holding tight to a single phrase**: The reference here is to the practice of meditating single-mindedly on a single phrase, or huatou, such as "What was my original face before my parents were born?"

37. **insufficiently virile**: Chan texts often speak of the need for a person engaged in certain times of intensive meditation to demonstrate a "masculine" (*zhangfu*) strength and determination.

    Good and bad, right and wrong / are not up to me: Under a bright sky, justice should prevail but, unfortunately, during times of chaos there is little one can do about it. Here, Zhang may be referring to her chaotic thoughts, which she finds she cannot control despite her best efforts.

38. **And snatch away the pearl / under the dragon's neck**: Originally a parable from *Zhuangzi* referring to someone who is willing to take great risks in their greed for acquiring something valuable. In Chan texts, it refers to the need to take risks to obtain the jewel of enlightenment.

39. The eight sufferings (*ba ku*) refer to the sufferings associated with: (1) birth, (2) old age, (3) illness, (4) death, (5) separation from what one likes, (6) meeting what one doesn't like, (7) not getting what one wants, and (8) getting what one does not want (or in some lists, as the suffering inherent in the five aggregates). The word translated as "cream" here is *ghee*, often used in Buddhist texts as a metaphor for the highest expression of the teachings.

40. **And can now finally return home / to my father and mother!**: That is, returning to one's original Buddha nature after having "decapitated" the enemy of ignorance and self-delusion. There is also an indirect allusion to the story of the woman warrior Mulan, who returns to her parents after years spent on the battlefield.

41. **clothed in green lotus leaves**: There is a famous verse by the Tang dynasty Chan master Damei Fachang (752–839), the first couplet of which in translation reads, "My lotus ponds provide an endless supply of leaves robes; with my pine trees, I have a surplus of seeds for food." CBETA X80, no. 1565, 76b14–15.

42. **Emptiness, Provisional, and the Center**: The "triple truth" of

Tiantai Buddhism: (1) that all things (dharmas) are *empty* of any fixed and essential reality; (2) that they nevertheless have a temporary or provisional existence; and (3) they are both unreal and temporarily existing—that is, they are in the middle. These three truths are mutually inclusive and together constitute the absolute truth of reality.

***Calming and Contemplation* sutras**: *The Great Calming and Contemplation Treatise* (*Mohe zhiguan*) is a major text written by Zhiyi (538–597), traditionally regarded as the founder of the Tiantai school of Chinese Buddhism.

ultimate reality: Literally, the true or ultimate reality as experienced by the Buddha.

43. Three major commentaries and five minor works on the *Lotus Sutra* are all attributed to Zhiyi.

44. The *Vinaya of the Southern Mountain* (*Nanshan lu*) was compiled by Daoxuan (596–667) and became the basis for what is known as the Southern Mountain Vinaya school of Chinese Buddhism. The *Four Agama Sutras* refers to the first four collections of discourses in the Pali Buddhist canon.

45. **If you fail to unfasten the bell / from the neck of the tiger**: Based on the story of a brave soul who managed to hang a bell around the neck of a fierce tiger so that people would be alerted to its presence and seek safety. This later became a phrase found in many Chan texts. The most famous is associated with Chan Master Fayan Wenyi (885–958), who one day asked his disciples, "Who

can untie and remove the gold bell tied around the tiger's neck?" None of his monks were able to reply. Then a young boy, known for his naughty behavior, piped up and said, "It has to be the one who tied it around the tiger's neck in the first place." Upon hearing this response, Fayan indicated his approval.

Yuansongs and Tangpoems: That is, the songs (*qu*) of the Yuan dynasty (1271–1368) and the poems (*shi*) of the Tang dynasty (618–907).

46. A seminal section of Asaṅga's *Bodhisattvabhumi*.
47. According to legend, the flower of the *udumbara* (a type of fig tree) blooms only once every three thousand years and is thus used as a metaphor for rare events, such as the coming of a buddha.
48. **stirred the well waters**: Stirring up the water in the well is often used as a metaphor for emotions that disturb one's inner tranquility.
49. **books of immortality**: Although normally these would refer to Daoist writings, here they would appear to refer to Buddhist books that speak of a different sort of "immortality."

    carefree and unconcerned: This may possibly be an allusion to a phrase appearing in Yongming Yanshou's *Records of the Source Mirror*: "Encountering situations with understanding, even seeing colors and hearing sounds can lead to enlightenment. When the flowers flutter and the bracelets move, they can all settle the spirit." CBETA T48, no. 2016, 670a21–22.
50. **offer a water contemplation**: In the *Surangama Sutra* there are

descriptions of practitioners who contemplate water and subsequently go into a trancelike state, during which they become water both inside and out.

And when taken in, concealed / on the tip of a hair: A paraphrase of a line from the commentary by the great neo-Confucian philosopher Zhu Xi (1130–1200) on the *Doctrine of the Mean* (*Zhongyong*), an important Confucian classic attributed to the grandson of Confucius. Speaking of this text's essential principle, Zhu Xi writes, "If it is released, it encompasses the entire universe; if rolled up, then it retreats and hides in secrecy." Here, however, Zhang appears to be referring to the Buddhadharma.

51. **eons**: The term *jie*, used here, can refer to kalpas or eons but also to delusions or attachments.
52. **notes of a song**: Literally, the proper alteration of musical modes.
53. **I roam without a care**: "Xiaoyou" (Roaming carefree) is the title of the first chapter of the Daoist classic *Zhuangzi* and illustrates the ideal of the liberated person.
54. This line is a quote from the famous story, originally found in *Mencius*, about the farmer who tried to encourage his corn to grow by pulling at it and thus destroying it.
55. These guidelines, still popular among practitioners today, can be found in a letter written by Hanshan Deqing to a lay follower. See "To Chan Person Guanzhi Yun"(*Shi Guanzhi Yun chanren*) in *Laoren mengyouji* [The collected works of the Oldan's dream wanderings], CBETA X73, no. 1456, 489a9–22.

56. **Emptied-out guts:** *Kuchang*, originally referring to a state of hunger, is also used metaphorically to refer (negatively) to a state of creative depletion and (positively) to a deep meditative state free of thoughts. The latter is probably meant here.
57. This poem is identical to the poem included in "Sketches of Daily Life," p. 43.
58. **spiky chestnuts**: While the flesh of the chestnut is very sweet, its prickly skin makes it difficult to swallow. This is a metaphor used in Chan texts to point to the difficulty of practice, in particular koan practice.

    tracks on the snow: In one of his poems, the great Song dynasty poet Su Shi, also known as Su Dongpo (1037–1101), compares human life to a wild goose who walks on the snow, which momentarily retains its tracks while the goose flies off into the unknown.
59. Jichan (1852–1912) was also known as Jing'an and, more familiarly, the Eight-Fingered Monk. For more about this modern poet-monk, see Jason Protass, "The Plum-Blossom Monk: Jichan" in *Buddhist Masters of Modern China*, ed. Benjamin Brose (Shambhala, 2025), 219–247.
60. Jiannan is the Song dynasty poet Lu You (1125–1210). Actually, the original source of the first line is a poem by Du Fu, while the second line would appear to be from a poem by the Qing dynasty poet Huang Jingren (1749–1783).
61. Jiyin is Huihong Juefan (also known as Huihong Dehong, 1071–1128).

62. "samadhi of play" is a free and untrammeled state of playfulness, said to issue naturally from enlightenment.
63. The Lotus Samadhi ritual is an extended ritual practice associated primarily with the Tiantai school. For more on Zhang's experience with the Lotus Samadhi practice, see Beata Grant, "Tiantai Master Benkong," in Brose, ed., *Buddhist Masters of Modern China*, 175–96.
64. This is a couplet from a poem, entitled "Morning Hunger: For Zilu," that Lu You (also known as Lu Fangwen, 1125–1210) wrote for his youngest son. This poem, written while living in exile, speaks of living in a hut in a remote mountain village and waking up with a stomach rumbling with hunger.
65. The Tang poet and painter Wang Wei (701–761), a Buddhist layman, would often retreat to his country estate, the Wangchuan Villa, for periods of quiet reclusion.
66. The Tang poet Du Fu (also known as Du Zimei) and his famous Thatched Cottage in Chengdu, Sichuan.
67. The Tang poet Bai Juyi (also known as Bai Letian, 772–846) had a hermitage on Mount Lu where he would engage in Pure Land Buddhist devotional practice.
68. The name of the Loyang residence of Shao Anle (also known as Shao Yong, 1012–1077), an important neo-Confucian philosopher and poet greatly influenced by Buddhism.
69. In a famous essay, Tao Yuanming refers to himself as the Master of Five Willows, because of the five willow trees around his home in the countryside.

70. The famous Buddhist lay teacher Mahasattva Fu (497–569) supported himself and his family by fishing, until one day he met an Indian monk and was converted to Buddhism. He then took up residence in a simple thatched hut beneath two pine trees at the foot of Mount Song, in Henan province. Mount Song is traditionally associated with Bodhidharma.
71. The Buddhist layman Liu Yiming (352–410) was one of the early members of the White Lotus Society founded on Mount Lu in Jiangsu province by the eminent monk Huiyuan (334–416). This society was dedicated to the practice of the recitation of the name of Amitabha Buddha and the aspiration for rebirth in the Western Pure Land.
72. **gulls as companions**: Befriending a gull is a common trope found in the Chinese poetry of seclusion. It represents the guileless innocence of a child, from a famous anecdote in *Zhuangzi*. Literally, let others call me an ox or a horse. This passage comes from *Zhuangzi*, in the chapter "The Way of Heaven" (*Tiandao*). See Burton Watson, trans., *The Complete Works of Zhuangzi* (Columbia University Press, 2013), 105.
73. **Worldly affairs**: An allusion to the lines from a famous poem by the Song dynasty poet Zhu Dunru (1081–1159), which read, "The affairs of the world are as brief as a spring dream; human feelings are as thin as autumn clouds."
74. **Holding fast to the sharp sword**: An example of this concept is Moye, the name of a legendary double-edged sword said to have been forged during the tumultuous Spring and Autumn period

(ca. 771–256 B.C.E.). Legendary swords such as this are often used as symbols of the unwavering courage of heroes fighting for their country. Here it may refer to the heroic determination required of Chan practitioners, and perhaps also to the sharp sword of discriminative wisdom needed to vanquish the demons of delusion.

75. **Yellow millet**: A reference to a popular story about a young scholar who stops at an inn on his way to take the civil examinations. While waiting for the yellow millet porridge the innkeeper is preparing for his meal, he falls asleep and in a dream experiences all the ups and downs, wins and losses, of an entire lifetime. Upon waking, he finds the millet porridge is still not ready but that he himself has come to realize the vanity of worldly pursuits. He then decides to set out in search of the Way.
76. While the precepts based on the *Brahma's Net Sutra* were the most used in China, in the early twentieth century a number of teachers and Buddhist masters preferred the precepts drawn from the *Bodhisattvabhumi* of the *Yogacarabhumi-sastra*, which they believed to be more authentically Indian, more closely adherent to Mahayana Buddhism, and more suitable for use by both monastic and laypersons living in modern times.
77. The name of a central chapter of the *Bodhisattvabhumi*, composed in Sanskrit in the late fourth century by the Indian philosopher-sage Asanga, the founder of the Yogacara school of Mahayana Buddhism. It addresses the questions of how to judge and validate knowledge, and how confusions about "reality" arise.

78. This passage can be found in the *Chronicles of the Sangha Jewel in the Forests of Chan* (*Chanlin senbao zhuan*), a compilation of Chan biographies by the Song dynasty monk Huihong. See CBETA X79, no. 1560, 504c8–11.

Miscellaneous Verses on Gaya

1. There are actually thirty-five poems in the series, but the two that appear also in *Experiments in a Life of Farming-Chan* are not included here.
2. There is an allusion here to a four-line verse by the poet-monk and recluse Shiwu Qinggong (1272–1352). The first couplet of this verse describes the beauties of the lake and mountain near where he lives. The second couplet in translation reads, "What you see before your eyes has always been the reality / What need to *gassho* and ask the old Chan master?" See the *Records of Shiwu Qinghong of Fuyuan* (*Fuyuan Shiwu Qinghong chanshi lu*), CBETA X70, no. 1399, 668c19–20.
3. There is possibly an allusion here to the story in chapter 79 of the *Avatamsaka Sutra*, where Bodhisattva Samantabhadra snaps his fingers before the hall of Maitreya and that door opens for him to enter. The Gate of Mystery refers to the Buddhist path.
4. **antelope is hanging by its horns**: Chan Master Xuefeng Yicun (822–908) compared the search for a method leading to enlightenment to a hunter's dog sniffing out its prey. The experience of

enlightenment, however, was not to be found in this way, and he compared it to how the antelope, according to traditional Chinese belief, would avoid being caught in this way by hanging itself from a tree by its horns, leaving no scent on the ground.

5. **Who is the host . . . the essence-function**: The metaphors of guest and host are often used in Buddhist texts to indicate the relationship between teacher and student, or more abstractly, between objective and subjective viewpoints. "Essence-function" refers to the relationship between the fundamental substance of things, often hidden, and their visibly manifest aspects or activities.
6. **Hiding talents, covering traces**: In Chinese, this is an idiom meaning to conceal one's talents and bide one's time.
7. **A single steed**: In chapter 2 of the *Zhuangzi*, titled "Discussion on Making All Things Equal," we find the following passage: "To use an attribute to show that attributes are not attributes is not as good as using a non-attribute to show that attributes are not attributes. To use a horse to show that a horse is not a horse is not as good as using a non-horse to show that a horse is not a horse, Heaven and earth are one attribute; the ten thousand things are one horse." Burton Watson, trans., *The Complete Works of Zhuangzi* (Columbia University Press, 2013), 10.

   three mysteries: The ninth-century Chan master Linji Yixuan's "three mysteries" are the mystery contained in the essence, the mystery contained in the word, and finally the mystery in the mystery.

Elder: Literally "Old Man" or "Old Fellow." Note that Zhang refers to herself in both this poem and the next (in calling herself a layperson) using male-gendered terms.

8. **I headed straight to the cliff / from where to let go**: A verse from Case 32 of Wumen Huikai's *Gateless Gate* uses four metaphors to describe the challenges of authentic Chan practice: walking on the edge of sword, going up a mountain of ice; not touching the stairs [while climbing them]; and letting go from the edge of cliff. See CBETA T48, no. 2005, 297b1–2.
9. **the two schools**: The Mainstream and Mahayana schools of Buddhism.

   ordinary know-nothing: That is, someone unschooled in Buddhist doctrine.
10. **All things have from the start / formed a single body**: This is a notion often found in Chan and neo-Confucian writings. The neo-Confucian philosopher Wang Yangming, for example, writes, "A great man is one who regards all things in heaven and earth as one, who sees all under heaven as a single family, and all within the country as a single person." *Wang Yangming quanji* [The complete works of Wang Yangming] (Shanghai guji chubanshe, 2011), 1066.

    five-colored fish: Traditionally considered to be a magical creature. Here it appears to refer to the glitz and glamour of worldly life.
11. **one single phrase:** A reference to the mantra NAMO AMITOFO, the single-minded chanting of which is believed by Pure Land Bud-

dhists to ensure rebirth in the Pure Land.

12. **remedies**: Presumably, the medicine that will cure her worldly guests of their delusions.

    illness of Vimalakirti: In the *Vimalakirti Sutra*, Vimalakirti is described as having feigned illness, and when well-wishers came to inquire after his health, he engaged them in discussions about the Dharma.

13. **legs added to a snake**: To claim something that does not exist—that is, nonsense. Adding legs to a snake is an idiom used to refer to something that is superfluous.
14. **Twisted roots, tangled branches**: This expression is often used to refer to complicated matters that are difficult to resolve.

Thoughts on Injuring My Hand When Chopping Wood

1. **Thirty days and only nine meals**: A Chinese idiom that is often used to refer to the dire poverty suffered by those who chose to become recluses. Tao Qian, for example, in poem five of his series "Imitating the Ancients," writes, "Three ten-day periods with nine meals / in ten years I've worn only one cap."

Thoughts on Living in the Forest

1. The last line of this poem may refer to the end of the Second Sino-Japanese War in 1945. It may also be meant metaphorically—that is, a pause in inner mental turmoil.

2. **unborn**: The original nature of all things, which is not subject to birth and death.

Returning Home to Gaya Forest, Joyfully Written

1. No date is given for this poem, but it would appear to have been written when Zhang was in her late forties, shortly before her ordination.

BIBLIOGRAPHY

Baiting Xufa, ed. *Qixinlun shujihuiyue* [Commentary on *The Awakening of Faith*]. CBETA (Chinese Buddhist Electronic Text Association) X45, no. 768.

Benkong. *Yanshui ji* [Misty waters collection]. Yuan quan chubanshe. Yuanquan Publications, 1975. Reprinted in 1996.

Brose, Benjamin, ed. *Buddhist Masters of Modern China.* Shambhala, 2025.

Chanlin senbao zhuan [Chronicles of the Sangha Jewel in the Forests of Chan]. CBETA T48, no. 2016.

Grant, Beata. "Tiantai Master Benkong." In *Buddhist Masters of Modern China*, edited by Benjamin Brose, 175–196. Shambhala, 2025.

Grant, Beata. "Thirty Years of Dream-Wandering: The Conversion Narratives of Zhang Ruzhao (1900–1969)." *Nan Nü: Men, Women and Gender in China* 19, no. 1 (2017): 28–63.

Hanshan Deqing. *Laoren mengyouji* [The collected works of the Old Man Hanshan's dream wanderings]. CBETA X73, no. 1456.

Juefan Huihong. *Shimen wenzichan* [Literary Chan from Stone Gate Monastery]. CBETA J23, no. B135.

Lau, D. C., trans. *Mencius*. Penguin Books, 2003.

Shiwu Qinghong. *Fuyuan Shiwu Qinghong chanshi lu* [Discourse records of Shiwu Hong of Fuyuan]. CBETA X70, no. 1399.

Watson, Burton, trans. *The Analects of Confucius*. Columbia University Press, 2007.

Watson, Burton, trans. *The Complete Works of Zhuangzi*. Columbia University Press, 2013.

Yongming Yanshou. *Zongjing lu* [Records of the Source Mirror]. CBETA X79, no. 1560.

Zhang Lifa et al., eds. *Zhang Ruzhao Foxue zuopin ji* [Collected Buddhist writings of Zhang Ruzhao]. Shehui kexue wenxian chubanshe, 2020.

ABOUT THE TRANSLATOR

After teaching Chinese literature and culture for many years at Washington University in St. Louis, **BEATA GRANT** now lives in her home state of New Mexico. Her publications include *Daughters of Emptiness: Poetry of Buddhist Nuns of China* (Wisdom Publications, 2003); *Eminent Nuns: Female Chan Buddhist Masters of Seventeenth Century China* (University of Hawai'i Press, 2008); *Zen Echoes: Verse Commentaries by Three Female Chan Masters* (Wisdom Publications, 2017); and *An Anthology of Poetry by Buddhist Nuns of Late Imperial China* (Oxford University Press, 2023).